D0971049

Beyond
the
Fairway

Beyond the Fairway

Zen Lessons, Insights, and Inner Attitudes of Golf

Jeff Wallach

BANTAM BOOKS

New York   Toronto   London   Sydney   Auckland

WEST BEND LIBRARY

BEYOND THE FAIRWAY

A Bantam Book / May 1995

Grateful acknowledgment is made for permission to reprint from *Zen in the Art of Archery* by Eugen Herrigel copyright © 1953 by Pantheon Books, Inc. Reprinted by permission of Pantheon Books, a division of Random House, Inc.

All rights reserved.
Copyright © 1995 by Jeff Wallach
Cover art copyright © 1995 by Tom Hallman
Woodcuts copyright © 1995 by Dan Heitkamp
Book design by Glen M. Edelstein
No part of this book may be reproduced or transmitted
in any form or by any means, electronic or mechanical,
including photocopying, recording, or by any information
storage and retrieval system, without permission in
writing from the publisher.
For information address: Bantam Books.

Library of Congress Cataloging-in-Publication Data

Wallach, Jeff.
Beyond the fairway : Zen lessons, insights, and inner attitudes of
golf / Jeff Wallach.
p. cm.
ISBN 0-553-37333-1
1. Golf—Psychological aspects. 2. Golf—Miscellanea.
3. Wallach, Jeff. I. Title.
GV979.P75W35 1995

796.352'01—dc20   94-31039
CIP

Published simultaneously in the United States and Canada

Bantam Books are published by Bantam Books, a division of Bantam Doubleday Dell
Publishing Group, Inc. Its trademark, consisting of the words ''Bantam Books'' and the
portrayal of a rooster, is Registered in U.S. Patent and Trademark Office and in other
countries. Marca Registrada. Bantam Books, 1540 Broadway, New York, New York 10036.

PRINTED IN THE UNITED STATES OF AMERICA

BVG 01

796.352
W 155

For my parents,
Rosemay and Sidney Wallach, with love and gratitude.

Contents

CONTENTS

INTRODUCTION

Beyond the Fairway

M Y FIRST GOLF MEMORY IS AS CLEAR TO ME AS MY OWN name—spelled out in bold black letters—at the top of the leader board in the U.S. Open of my dreams: I was eight years old, and we were visiting my grandparents in Florida during spring vacation. On an afternoon when nothing had been planned for my brother and me and we'd tired of playing shuffleboard and laughing at the old men in Bermuda shorts and white patent leather shoes with dark socks, our dad rescued us from imminent trouble by taking us out to a pitch-and-putt golf course just off Collins Avenue in Miami Beach. It was late in the day, and the tropical sky was threatening. Palm fronds danced crazily in a wind, and soon thunder and lightning would roll in off the slate-gray ocean.

The tiny golf course was ragged and weird (characteristics I would learn to love many years later), built up with brown mounds that were supposed to emulate the rolling terrain of a Scottish links in miniature, set among the high rises and strip malls of south Florida. It was the kind of place where they handed you a wedge and a putter when you paid your greens fee. We were the only people out on the course.

It must have been around the sixth hole. My brother, who was already a good athlete at age thirteen, and my dad, who had always been one, teed off. I took a few full misses at my own bruised Titleist, and then sculled a slow grounder fifty yards into a sand trap next to the green. A good shot, for me.

As we walked down the fairway, my brother shook his head disapprovingly and suggested that I just pick up, since I would never hit my ball out of the trap. I looked at my father, who glanced at the darkening sky and then handed me his own sand wedge. "Try to hit two inches behind the ball," he advised with totally unfounded confidence, an unreasonable optimism that only a father could express. Perhaps if I'd said that I needed to meet up with a B-movie starlet in a hotel in Los Angeles that very night, he would have handed me the keys to his Buick: My dad implicitly believed in his boys.

I nodded and smiled as I took the wedge. I walked into the middle of the trap, as the men of my family looked on and scattered raindrops fell. I drew the club back and swung it with all the awkwardness of a nonathlete. Yet I understood exactly how this shot was supposed to work. It made complete sense to me to hit behind the ball and follow through with exaggerated momentum.

Sand flew off the club face, and in that frozen moment when I looked up, I saw several things at once: my father grinning widely in approval; my brother, standing behind the green and laughing because he thought I'd hit only sand; and the perfect white smiling sphere of my ball climbing, floating, ascending over the lip of the trap. It landed on the gauzy Bermuda grass and rolled to a stop three feet from the pin.

If I were a touring pro writing his memoirs, this particular anecdote might have ended with me holing out and proceeding from that experience to a career filled with great golf shots that would highlight how I overcompensated for my early, uncoordinated years by excelling at the sport.

This is not a golfing memoir, which is another way of saying that I'm still an eighteen handicap. But it's precisely in the fact that I *didn't* instantly master the game (and still haven't) that the real story occurs; it's in the fact that a clumsy eight-year-old who wouldn't come into his own for another two decades could hit a perfect golf shot, and then spend the ensuing years trying to duplicate the experience, truly believing that he could always become something far greater than he was on any given day, somehow comprehending all along that nearly everything he really needed to know about golf was already inside him.

Although I was too young to understand it as such, I experienced a deeply transcendent moment on that scrubby golf course in Florida. There hadn't been time to think about how important it was to hit a great shot or, as I do now, to fiddle with my grip and try to remember the advice (often conflicting) of a dozen different pros who've offered me tips over the years. There wasn't room to consider how a great shot might elicit my brother's approval, please my father, and make me— even for an instant, but an instant I wouldn't soon forget—a star. The event was this pure: I understood how the shot should work, which left only the execution of it. And when you're so sure of something, to the exclusion of all other possible outcomes—when you're not even conscious of the act or its consequences—there can be only one result. I hit the perfect shot.

Many years later, the same kind of thing happened to me while I was playing at Poppy Hills on the California coast with an old college friend, a five handicap who, at age thirty, claimed to be training for the senior tour. I'd been playing badly all day. I'd already launched half a dozen balls into the graceful, innocent Monterey pines, and was embarrassed by my performance. But on the final three holes, when I was far beyond caring whether I scored well, something clicked: I strung together a series of long, straight, accurate shots, and finished with birdies to card a nearly respectable 95. The sudden purity of my swing was trying to tell me something, and I knew that if I examined this phenomenon long enough, the skies would cleave open above me and I'd reach some sort of deep understanding—like Zen monks, who spend years studying koans (ancient, mystical parables) to achieve a moment of revelation. Golf, I knew, could provide insight into the truer aspects of experience. In that way, the game is like an out-of-body experience, or truly memorable sex.

When golf first became a metaphor to me, I believed that if I could only *control* my game, I could necessarily exert the same kind of discipline and control in other areas of my life. But, of course, I achieved that temporary perfection on the last few holes at Poppy Hills because I *let go* of control, of trying to impress my friend—it seemed too late for that— and because I was no longer concerned with shooting a round that I could brag about later. If I'd looked more closely at that early sand shot in Florida or my string of birdies at Poppy

Hills, I might have recognized that the game was really trying to teach me the opposite lesson: to transcend control, to lose consciousness of everything. Only then might I play—and live—purely. When I stopped caring about such specific and limited goals as my score, when I surrendered to the process and just *played*, I began truly to experience and enjoy each shot, and I began scoring better.

Therein lies the timeless beauty of golf: that as I grow older it reveals more of itself, and I continue to descend to deeper levels of meaning. Over twenty years of play, the game has offered many rewards on many levels. It's offered perspective on myself and a distraction from the loneliness of writing. It's introduced me to many wonderful, strange, obsessive people (as well as a few annoying folks who throw their clubs and always seem to be clearing their throats while you putt), and helped maintain a friendship or two. It's provided a good reason to get outside, to enjoy and sometimes challenge the weather, to stand under a leafy tree waiting for a rainstorm to pass, to stay out after dark when the stars first pop out, to wake early or skip lunch or act impractically or with abounding silliness, to dream and to want something small and yet vastly important—such as the occasional birdie—that might connect me to other people, other places, and other selves, all linked together by swaths of green grass warming in the sun.

In recent years I've come to experience the game at an even deeper level, where it shares much in common with Eastern philosophy and is closely related to the spiritual practice of Zen. I've come to see golf as a sort of koan (or series of koans), the serious consideration of which often reveals something intrinsically true about some subject that has nothing to do with the game. Zen koans are designed to shake students out of their limited, subjective perceptions so that suddenly, in a flash of insight, they see in a new way and eventually achieve true enlightenment. Such understanding is not based on logic or intellection, and requires an intuitive leap.

Of everything that golf has taught me, the most valuable lesson has been about the tremendous advantages of moving beyond the fairway to other levels—past the stereotypical surface manifestations of golf and of everything else, past what is obvious and superficial, past subjective reality, and into deeper realms. These physical, metaphorical, and metaphysical movements into what I call the game's unmanicured terrain—which manifests itself in unlimited ways and constantly surprises me with new ones—lead toward everything that golf *can* be. This territory awaits beyond the apparent, literal surface of the golf koan, which can reveal lessons of great depth and power despite its appearance as a simple story.

Within the confines of a single round of golf, we unequivocally strive to avoid hitting our golf balls beyond the fairway, which is to say outside the predictable, well-maintained territory of the golf course: into tall, untended grass (where we might lose *ourselves* as well as our balls), into woods or lakes, into the living room of some condo built along a resort course, or into the parking lot of an adjacent office complex. But we might also *find* our balls—and ourselves—in such locations.

While hitting beyond the fairway implies a lack of control (yes, that is the point!), it also represents a movement beyond established perceptions and limitations. When players step into unmanicured terrain, golf becomes an adventure sport and a spiritual journey. When we move beyond the obvious and visible into the unknown, a round of golf enters the realm of adventure travel and mysticism, both out in the world and inside ourselves. When we no longer fear crossing over the edge into the rough or feel the pressure to land where we're supposed to, we become truly free. Anything can happen, and often does. When golf becomes an expedition where the traveling and not the destination matters most, it may reveal possibilities that never occurred to us. When we distinguish between golf (the sport) and golfing (the action, the process, the journey), and once we understand a golf koan—in fact, once we recognize the game *as* koan—we've already entered that realm beyond the fairway.

I have many friends and companions who've never understood golf as anything more than the pastime of men who stand around discussing mortgage rates as they line up their putts. Sure, I've actually met such players—"serious" golfers who discuss the private clubs and posh resorts where they play and the famous teachers with whom they take lessons as a way to set themselves apart and above. They are like the tourists in our national parks who drive in, take a snapshot of a mountain or waterfall, and drive out, thinking they've "experienced" Yosemite or Crater Lake or the Grand Canyon. Many people unfairly attribute this kind of shallowness (and elitism) to all golfers and hate the game for that reason. But in fact, such attitudes indicate a profound ignorance of what golf truly is: an activity that can unite very different people in the great Oneness.

Thankfully, legions of us know that golf is much, much more than a game, especially *that* game of shallowness and posing. It's become, for some folks, a four-hour religious pilgrimage, a motivation to travel, a component of a personal vision of the world. Such golfers play for fun, but we also recognize the inherent possibilities; we welcome the infinite

variety of potential occurrences, from the serendipitous instance when our drive hits the cart path and bounces over a
bunker, or ricochets off a tree and onto the green, to the true
grace of a hole-in-one. We open ourselves to the places golf
can take us. We play because of the chance—on every shot—
for transcendence and redemption. We know that, ultimately,
the game can transport us beyond the fairway to where everything converges.

Geographically, unmanicured terrain exists beyond patently
familiar destinations: at a dusty layout sprawling across the
Warm Springs Indian Reservation in the high desert of
Oregon, where two young hairdressers drink tequila shots in
the bar, or at a dirt venue hacked into the foothills of the
Himalayas in Nepal. Unmanicured terrain thrives during a
glow-ball competition played beneath a pitch-black, star-flaked
night sky, or at the annual Midnight Sun Tournament, which
takes place in Fairbanks, Alaska, on the evening of the summer
solstice, like some pagan ritual honoring the triumph of light
over darkness. Unmanicured terrain manifests itself in a make-
shift competition invented during a wilderness rafting adventure on Idaho's Salmon River and conducted with a bent
Ponderosa pine bough and two stream-rounded stones.

Metaphorically, unmanicured terrain can exist even at the
center of the most conservative bastions of the game, as a
perspective or state of mind. It lives in the spirit of communion
on famous Scottish golf links; it draws breath from a man who
has spent his life engineering new dimple patterns on golf balls
to make them fly farther. Traveling to this territory may be
as simple as looking at what some detail really implies—by

noticing, for example, that while a father and son play golf together, much more than a golf game may be taking place between them.

Metaphysically, unmanicured terrain often extends outward through more cosmic, philosophical considerations. Journeying there may require relinquishing a long-held belief—for instance, that golf is a game of control—and learning how to perceive reality differently. It may require viewing the game as an artistic pursuit or discipline. Zen students often take up such disciplines as archery, painting, swordsmanship, or flower arranging and use these vehicles to help transport them toward enlightenment. By pursuing these activities, a student can learn to focus intently yet lose consciousness of his efforts so that his actions become pure and egoless. Thus, the archer becomes the target, and the golfer learns to "be the ball." Yet even if golf becomes, for you, a spiritual pursuit, don't lose sight of the fact that it is just one of many pursuits, and what matters is the process of revealing, not the activity that facilitates the process. It is the excursion itself and not the destination that is important.

Michael Murphy took us for a trip through this metaphysical territory in his book *Golf in the Kingdom,* but you don't have to travel to a mythical golf club in Scotland and stay up all night in a ravine to find a place where golf and philosophy merge. While *Golf in the Kingdom* distilled the essence of golf from a personal and particular mystical experience, we can all discover this terrain during our own golf rounds once we begin to see the game in a new way.

Of course, some players will be happy just to learn something previously unseen, while others may energetically pursue golf to its most esoteric and philosophical depths—

which is a way of saying that the game offers something for everyone.

The chapters that follow provide a variety of golf stories and experiences that you might choose to see as koans; each is meant to give you a new perspective on the game. Just as Zen Masters offer their students different koans to elicit different levels of understanding, the chapters also offer various levels of insight. Some simply reveal a dimension that lies barely beneath the surface. Some specifically address particular Eastern concepts such as transcendence, visualization, discipline, or meditation. A few ambitiously point the way toward enlightenment. Mostly, though, these chapters offer examples of how you might begin to view your own golf experiences as personal koans capable of revealing something deeper. Learn not to see the grains of sand in a bunker, for instance, but rather the spaces between them.

My intention is to present a new way of seeing golf, which in turn may help you to use golf as a new way of seeing. Coincidentally, learning some of the inherent metaphysical lessons may improve your game by helping you plug into your own capabilities, and by tapping into the Oneness of all things. At this level, golf exists as a kind of golden circle, because the greatest teachings of Eastern philosophy—transcending conscious thoughts of good and bad, difficult and easy; living purely in the moment, without the distracting chatter of subjectivity—are the very lessons that can make you a better golfer.

To facilitate this shift in perception, and to help you depart from the fairway and head out into unmanicured terrain, I've begun each chapter with at least one short epigraph—often a

koan—meant to startle you into another viewpoint and resonate through the story that follows. Some are taken directly
from Eastern teachings. In others, Zen students may recognize
the kernels of ancient Zen stories that I've translated into a
language that golfers are fluent in; I've transformed monks into
assistant pros, the monastery into a country club, and gathered
the wisdom possessed by myriad Zen Masters and bestowed it
upon the Head Pro. The Eastern lessons, however, remain
intact, and seem to me to offer a mysterious synchronicity and
harmony when juxtaposed with the golf tales they introduce.

The book begins with a few stories describing very traditional golf destinations and experiences in surprising ways. It
moves outward from there, skirting the edges of the familiar,
describing things just beyond the traditional venues and values
of golf. The final stories range even further out; they communicate from way off in the deep grass, woods, and swamp-
lands. They'll transport you to bizarre, unexpected locations
and recount events that epitomize this notion of golf as adventure, as journey, and as koan.

Ultimately, though, this book isn't so much *about* Zen or
other Eastern philosophies as it is full of examples of them.
Because, as the Masters say, once you talk about a thing directly, you've already lost it.

I've tried to lay out the following chapters like a well-
designed golf course, built into the terrain of my own experiences as a player and golf journalist. Because a couple grew
out of much simpler magazine travel pieces, I've left in some
of the original travel information; it may prove helpful if
you're planning a trip and also provides some context to explain what in the world I was doing playing golf in places such
as Alaska and Thailand, Africa and Nepal. But in this book

these pieces now reveal the Eastern dimension of the game and its venues, which commercial magazines don't often find appropriate or even comprehensible.

Finally, this book is for golfers who love the sport but not its sedentary stereotypes and surface manifestations. It doesn't teach you how to shave strokes off your handicap, since I have enough trouble remembering to shift my own weight. It may help you, however, by revealing a new kind of attitude, thereby giving you an inner game that is more likely to help with your outer swing.

This book is for players who might search for balls in the rough out of the sheer joy of potential discovery; who feel that taking a penalty stroke is somehow a breach of morality, an opportunity lost; who would rather stumble upon a moose in the woods than hit a dead-center drive; who measure a great round less by their score than by the overall experience.

Flip through these pages as you dream about an upcoming golf vacation or the approaching season at your own country club. Share some of these stories—or your own—with your partners as you wait to tee off on the first hole. I hope you'll recognize from reading about my experiences that there's so much more to the game than what appears obvious from the fairways, and that you'll learn truly to love the rough (even in the desert, where you may need to watch out for rattlesnakes). As you sit back and read this on a long flight or in a favorite lounge chair imprinted with the shape of your own life, I hope the book will remind you of the sweet scent of freshly cut grass, the crisp *thwok* of a club cleanly hitting a ball, and the feel of walking toward the eighteenth green in the fading light of a warm autumn afternoon.

Beyond
the
Fairway

PART ONE

Zen Perspectives from the Fairway: Old Doglegs, New Tricks

CHAPTER ONE

Well-Connected Golfing in Scotland

Before a person studies Zen, mountains are mountains and waters are waters; after a first glimpse into the truth of Zen, mountains are no longer mountains and waters are not waters; after enlightenment, mountains are once again mountains, and waters once again waters.

—Zen saying

A new member of the golf club was anxious to learn about the course and said: "I have only recently become a member. Will you be gracious enough to show me the way to the first tee?"

The Head Pro said: "Do you hear the murmuring of the stream?"

The new member said: "Yes, I do."

The Head Pro said: "Here is the entrance."

—Zen golf koan

BEYOND THE FAIRWAY

PRESTWICK . . . ROYAL TROON . . . TURNBERRY . . . NORTH
Berwick.

Carnoustie. Gullane. Royal Dornoch. Nairn.

The names of Scottish golf courses are like mantras to me
now. They roll off my tongue with a cool liquidity, like clear
water running over smooth stones. Sometimes I whisper these
names aloud, and they transport me beyond the overstylized,
ultramanicured, artificial fairways of American golf, connecting
me to the pure spirit from which the game was first distilled.

Late one October, when northern climes were spinning toward winter but the afternoons were still golden with syrupy
light, I spent eight sylvan days chasing an elusive golf dream
across the dunes and fescue grasses, the heather and gorse of
Scottish links courses, searching for connection, seeking out
the lost and achingly beautiful heart of the game—in which I
only half believed. For much of my life I've felt, intuitively,
that golf could connect me to pure, clear streams of consciousness, but I'd never quite discovered how to enter the
flow. One fall I set out for the headwaters of the game, to
drink from that true source and discover what it could teach
me.

My days went much like this: On a Friday morning, for
example, I woke early in my suite at the Turnberry Hotel and
looked out the window as light gathered over the Firth of
Clyde and shadows retreated from the championship Ailsa
course (which I'd played the previous day) stretching greenly
beside the windy dunes below. The lighthouse perched on the
cliffs beside the ninth hole shone like a white monolith in the
rising sun, and beyond, the peaks of Arran sketched a blue
line against the horizon.

Downstairs, in the dining room, I opened *The International*

Herald Tribune across the starched table linen and ate a full Scottish breakfast accompanied by strong coffee thick with cream. Then I called for my car and, as frost melted off the surrounding countryside, drove north too fast along winding roads to the small town of Prestwick. The leaves on the trees were yellow and ragged against the bluing sky, and the fields were brown and gold, dusted with white. In the small towns through which I drove, children in blue uniforms walked to school along the narrow streets.

At the old stone clubhouse of the Prestwick Golf Club— home of the first Open Championship (which Americans call the British Open) in 1860—Secretary David Donaldson took me for more strong coffee in the private card room, where century-old portraits of captains and secretaries stared menacingly down from the walls and antique golf clubs and scorecards from famous matches were displayed in glass cases.

As we waited for the morning chill to burn off, Donaldson and I compared notes on various far-flung golfing destinations; he seemed to have played on every continent except Antarctica. An hour later, my host summoned two caddies and we headed out to play eighteen of the most diverse and unique golf holes gathered together on a single course anywhere— holes requiring long, blind shots over monstrous dunes and quarries of sand, laid out along ancient stone fences and speckled with bunkers so deep you'd need a Ph.D. in philosophy just to see bottom. And all of it threaded delicately by the murmuring, meandering waters of Pow Burn.

We played a friendly match as Donaldson told me stories and my caddy, Waldo, produced a few gems of commentary. After I hit a long drive off the fourth tee, he observed, ''Some people don't go that far on holiday.''

As Donaldson and I were struggling up the dune that gave the fifth hole, Himalaya, its name, I asked him who had designed this fabulous course.

"God," he said without missing a beat, then added, "with a little help from Old Tom Morris."

I won our match seven and six after carding three pars in a row to open the back nine, and my opponent observed with acerbic humor that I must be a very good eighteen handicap. When we'd completed the round, we changed into coats and ties back at the clubhouse and drank a cocktail in the Smoke Room; my pint of lager arrived in a silver cup from the 1929 club championship. Then we lunched at a long table laid with fine silver in the formal dining room. Following a plate of venison accompanied by a sturdy claret, which we enjoyed in the excellent company of several other club members, and having worked up a warm and comforting buzz, I changed back into my favorite wool sweater and went out for another eighteen holes on my own in the bracing wind, with the smoky scent of burning peat perfuming the air.

I concluded the round with a gaming birdie attempt—and a solid par—as the light flattened and a soothing lavender color spread across the sky. Following a hot pub dinner in town, I ended the day in a steaming bath in my suite back at the Turnberry Hotel, while below my window a ghostly figure in Scottish plaid played the bagpipes along the walkway and the last light disappeared over the distant firth.

In spite of the almost religious cachet that Scotland holds for so many golfers, I'd tried not to expect anything too dramatic from my trip. Having grown up playing so much American golf, I always *wanted* to believe that a deeper game lay beyond the manicured fairways I was accustomed to. But I was afraid to trust this notion: I hate to be disappointed.

Eight days and 234 holes of golf on eleven different Scottish courses torpedoed my fears and taught me more about the game than I could have learned playing in America for another century. For starters, I realized that accessing golf's subtle inner core may require playing in swirling, howling salt air, lugging your own clubs up and down dunes for thirty-six holes, swinging helplessly at balls wedged in heather, tearing your clothes on gorse, freezing in cold ocean winds and occasional hail and sleet, and then giving yourself over to the reviving powers of a single-malt Highland whisky in the dark-paneled clubhouse bar overlooking a links where they've played golf for nearly five hundred years.

In America, we have so bastardized and diluted the game, manicured and modernized it, tidied it up and high-teched it, transformed it into an expensive, elitist hobby, and robbed it of so much of its purity and true character, it's a wonder we can draw any emotion from golf at all. Yet, at some level, we must still sense its inherent potential: Why else would so many of us become addicted?

By traveling to Scotland, I also learned that at its very heart, golf is a game of connections—to the land, to history, to community, and ultimately to ourselves. The game has a power to unite players in a kind of overarching Oneness, but to feel these connections, we must return to golf's roots and see where it was first played, and how, and maybe even why. In America we've severed the game's most powerful connections, so we must return home, to Scotland, to discover them again.

• • •

Some theories regarding the origins of golf posit that it evolved from early European ball-and-stick games such as Roman *paganica*, France's *jeu de mail*, or the Dutch game of *kolven*. Others claim that because Scotland's version was the first to employ a hole as a target, and because the Scots developed many of the rules we still follow today, they are the game's true progenitors.

Malcolm Campbell, writing in the *Random House International Encyclopedia of Golf*, offers an excellent description of how golf might have been born:

> One theory is that fishermen on the east coast of Scotland invented the game to amuse themselves as they returned home from their boats. What would be more natural than for a young fisherman, making his way across the rolling stretches of fine turf among the sand dunes, to pick up a stick of driftwood and aim a blow at a pebble? If he knocked the pebble forward, the competitive instinct inborn in man would demand that he hit it again to see if he could send it even farther. . . . It does not require a great leap of the imagination to develop that sense into a game between competing fishermen played across the links from boat to village, finishing at the same point each time, perhaps close to the local hostelry.

Although exactly how golf developed will remain a mystery, it seems certain that the game begins with and arises from the land. The ancient Scots must have found their rolling seaside links so deeply beautiful, so enticing, that they sought a more intimate relationship, a way of connecting to them—not through farming or construction or other intrusive, manipulative means, but in a gentler way that might intertwine them with the country in a timeless slow dance.

You need only gaze out over a golf course such as Royal Dornoch, in the remote northern highlands, to understand why folks might want to feel close to this terrain. From the seventh tee, suspended high upon the ridge of a dune, the land spreads receptively in gentle, undulating green mounds that spill out onto a wide, white sandy beach, which itself spills into the white-capped blue waters of Dornoch Firth and Embo Bay. Passively admiring such scenery is somehow not enough; you ache for a way of joining with the landscape, its colors and textures, its perfect though random lines, and for a way of hugging the coastline, rolling in the grass, burying yourself in the sand. As this earth is a goddess, you want more than just to love her from afar.

Hitting a golf ball (or a pebble) into that welcoming terrain projects us out into the landscape we so admire; it provides a way by which we can make the connection we crave. Just as children are compelled to throw stones into the rushing waters of a river, we propel a part of ourselves—energy and motion, power and form, hope and fear—by launching a golf ball skyward. We send this offering into the gorgeously welcoming natural world, which waits patiently to receive it. Searching for that ball leads us to explore the heart of the country. Finding the ball, we can project ourselves out again, toward a particularly lovely dune or a patch of blooming heather. Choosing a target merely lends direction to our aimless walk, provides a destination at which to point ourselves—although as the Scots well know, the destination doesn't matter nearly as much as the walking toward it.

When David Donaldson told me that God had designed the Prestwick golf course, he was completely serious. Scottish links bear few marks of human influence: no cart paths slice through the terrain, no fake million-dollar waterfalls distract the eye. The shrubbery doesn't spell out the name of a resort or corporation. No igloos, statues of elk, or giant plastic peanuts mark 150 yards to the green. If you were to pull the flag sticks out along a Scottish links course, you'd be hard pressed to identify it as a golf layout, in any way distinct from endless miles of seductive seaside terrain.

In America, on the other hand, we brutally hack golf courses out of the land. We design them mechanically, bulldoze and backhoe, and imprint a manufactured, self-conscious vision upon terrain that already possessed plenty of natural beauty and integrity of its own. Though often striking, American golf courses are artificially etched across deserts and wetlands; bolstered with bulkheads and railroad ties; built by rearranging land and rerouting or creating new watercourses; and planted with non-native turf. Sometimes immeasurably beautiful and balanced in the way that sculptures or landscape paintings may be beautiful, they are art. But in creating them, we sever our natural connection to the terrain.

Scottish links are the landscape itself—the source of and the inspiration for art. As a result of their wild, unmanicured terrain, Scottish golf courses are often more difficult to play. American golfers expecting the slate-flat fairway that lies so prevalent on U.S. courses may feel as if they've been beaten up. Links courses seem composed exclusively of up- or down- or side-hill lies and hundreds of evil, misanthropic bunkers that require proof of Scottish citizenship before letting you out.

The rough is no less unforgiving, consisting of waist-deep grasses, heather, and gorse. You'll find yourself making impossible promises if only a mishit ball will veer away from these nasty plants. Hitting out of heather is like trying to escape from an island prison. And gorse—sharp, thick, perennially disgruntled—is flora with an attitude. Both these hardy, individualistic plants assert their place in the natural setting, accept no excuses, and impose stiff penalties for disturbing them. Unless you're trying to learn something from such experiences, I advise avoiding heather and gorse at all costs— even if it means hitting wedges from tee to green.

And just in case the terrain and vegetation aren't uncompromising enough, the cold, salty, fierce wind whipping in off the ocean beside Scottish links courses has had plenty of room to gather momentum. You may have to lean into it just to stand up. It undermines your confidence, so you're afraid to give your shots over to it. Members of the Carnoustie Golf Club, on the northeastern coast, love to describe how during one Open Championship, Jack Nicklaus couldn't reach the green of one of the par threes with his *driver* during a strong blow. Gusts taunt and insult you until you give in to their antipathy and hit your shots beneath them, or give up and run for the clubhouse with your hands in the air.

As the *Tao Te Ching* says, "The receptive triumphs over the inflexible/The yielding triumphs over the rigid." The best players learn to adjust their games to accommodate earth, wind, vegetation, and the contours of a coast naturally shaped by rough weather; for example, you might consider developing

11

a low three-iron shot for distances of from sixty to two hundred yards. You'll also want a high-trajectory long-ball shot for the seemingly rare occasions when the wind is behind you. Such adaptability is not only a means of further connecting to the land, but has applications in many other areas of life outside of golf.

Of course, Scottish links are not completely devoid of man-made objects, though you're unlikely to come across many ball washers or wooden replicas of the holes. You *will* encounter stone walls, which establish a further sense of connection to the land and to history, both golf-related and otherwise. Many of these walls have lain across the seaside terrain for half a millennium, marking original property lines, or were built a couple of eons back to prevent sheep from wandering too far from home.

At the North Berwick Golf Club, I heard a caddy advise his American client to tee off with a mid-iron on one hole because a wall cut directly across the fairway, and the A position was to lay up short enough to have a clear second shot over the wall at the green.

"A wall? Are you sure?" the American asked.

"I'm pretty sure," the caddy responded. "It's been there for five hundred years."

In a few places, Scots have been playing golf across the same terrain—perhaps even across precisely the same layouts—for the same five hundred years, and some courses have remained virtually unchanged for more than a century. They ooze history.

Although Scots founded golf clubs at places such as Leith,

St. Andrews, Blackheath, and Burgess in the eighteenth century, records show that they'd already been playing in these locations for several hundred years. One bit of evidence survives in the form of documents recording fines meted out by the Church in the sixteenth century to men who were caught playing golf when they should have been attending religious services. In fact, Scots may actually have been pursuing their national passion since the fourteenth century.

It's worth noting that, besides the Church's objections to the game, national governments often banned ball-and-stick games because able-bodied men were pursuing them a bit too avidly in preference to martially practical activities such as archery. Could golf thereby have been indirectly responsible for early Scottish military losses? Perhaps this governmental grievance against the passion for nonwar games also explains in part why the links at Turnberry were converted into military runways during the world wars.

But golf is usually connected with Scottish history in less political ways. In the private dining room at the North Berwick Golf Club, for example, you might look up from your haggis and notice the wooden captain's board, with names dating back to 1832, when the club was founded. Visiting such places connects you to the game's history, but it may also make you feel as if untold generations of grumpy, critical old Scotsmen are peering over your shoulder and judging your every shot.

Many of the more established Scottish golf clubs also uphold formal traditions that bespeak their long history. At Prestwick, I learned rather suddenly, men are not allowed to enter the bar without a coat and tie. When I went to say good-bye to David Donaldson following my afternoon round there, I inadvertently walked into the Smoke Room in my sweater. Donaldson leapt to his feet and sped across the thick carpet as fast as I'd seen him move all day, whispering, "No. No. No," and holding up one hand as a signal for me to back away, as if I were about to step on a land mine or walk across the line of his birdie putt.

Scottish golfers also maintain their connection to history through the grand oral tradition, and every club possesses its own collection of historical anecdotes. On the first hole at Prestwick, Donaldson related this old club tale:

One afternoon a woman playing that same first hole sliced her tee shot over the stone boundary fence and out toward the railroad tracks beyond. At that very moment a train was rolling past, and her ball hit the solid metal side of the train and caromed back into the middle of the fairway. When the train slowed to a stop at the station platform, the conductor leaned out and called to her, "If it will be of any help, madam, I'll be passing by at the same time tomorrow."

Some clubs have even named course features after particularly memorable historic golf events. Hogan's Alley, at Carnoustie (where Scots have golfed since the sixteenth century), commemorates the spot along the sixth fairway where locals swear that during the Open Championship of 1953 Ben Hogan hit two such perfect tee shots into a narrow swath between bunkers and OB that his second-round shot landed in the divot from his first-round shot. At Prestwick, a yardage guide to the course calls a bunker on the sixteenth hole Willie Campbell's Grave, to mark the place where a competitor took four shots to get out of the sand, thereby ruining his chance to win the Open in 1884.

• • •

To Americans, anything that occurred in a previous decade seems historic, which is why many of us would give up a kidney to connect to Scotland's comparatively infinite golf history—particularly by playing the Old Course at St. Andrews, the official home of the Royal and Ancient Game. Being rather fond of both my kidneys, and unable to secure a personal reference from the Queen (practically a requirement for getting a tee time), I didn't play at St. Andrews during my visit to Scotland. But I can attest to the fact that the management there seems to have forgotten about Scotland's tradition of making golf accessible and egalitarian. Their attitude may well result from the influx of American visitors who haven't been content simply to vandalize the game at home, and have begun poisoning golf at its very roots.

American golf has long been considered an exclusive game because many of the best courses are either private or prohibitively expensive. While someone who actually works for a living was recently spotted playing an American layout, many of our best clubs and resorts are surrounded by high fences and security checkpoints. In spite of St. Andrews' haughty attitude, Scottish golf remains an accessible, communal activity that connects all types and classes of people. A few layouts still encompass parcels of land in the public domain, which means that town residents can graze their farm animals on some of the best fairways in the world. And in the middle of lining up your tee shot at courses such as Turnberry and North Berwick, don't be surprised if a few local residents cross the fairway in front of you on their way to stroll with their dogs along the seaside dunes. They may wave if they recognize another player in your foursome, or even stop to talk, lending

15

the links the feeling of a public square where members of the community go to meet.

Scottish golf's ability to encompass rather than divide the community is evident in their club memberships as well. At Carnoustie, I played thirty-six holes with a fireman who pays £180 a year (less than $300—what you might spend for a single day at an American golf resort) to play unlimited golf on one of the best courses in the world. He didn't have to face a complex, rigorous approval process, either; he just wrote them a check.

Caddies, of course, add to the sense of camaraderie and community on Scottish links. While caddies can prove particularly essential to visitors who haven't played a course before—a course that may demand blind shots and an unnatural, almost biblical familiarity with the tricky greens—they've also long been recognized as repositories of golf humor, wisdom, and philosophy, not to mention large quantities of beer. They're always happy to discourse on the subtle beauties of the game, and even more so when you're buying.

At Prestwick, after I knocked a tee shot onto the green of the par-three eleventh hole, my caddy, Waldo, reflected, "Happiness is a long walk with a putter."

At Royal Troon, I overheard a caddy continuously refer to his client's weak lags as "Mexican putts." After four or five such comments, the man finally said, "What in hell is a Mexican putt?"

"It's waiting for one more revolution," his caddy replied.

Scottish golf establishes its strong, direct connections to the land, to history, and to the community at large, at least partly by the manner in which Scottish golfers move across their very lovely and natural terrain: they *walk*. By walking, they interact directly with the terrain, play the game as it was meant to be played, and enjoy the opportunity to talk in a leisurely manner with the members of their foursome as they amble from tees to greens. Walking also adds a meditative aspect to the game, a chance for the individual to reflect between shots. In golfing eleven different courses throughout Scotland, I never glimpsed a single motorized cart.

While visiting Nairn Golf Club, northeast of Inverness, I played with three local members who debated this question of "buggies" as we sat over drinks in the clubhouse lounge. At the heart of their discussion was whether an eighty-year-old member who couldn't walk very well should be allowed to take out his own motorized cart. The vice-captain reasoned that playing golf might be keeping the old man alive, and perhaps they could make an exception in such a case. The former captain wondered whether they shouldn't require a doctor's note for players who couldn't walk the course. Their friend—who lacked any official title—pointed out that a few folks physically couldn't walk around the course because they were simply too fat. While the discussion didn't produce any specific conclusions, all three men agreed on two things: that golf was meant for walking, and that, as in America, buggies would only slow down play.

If anything should constitute a capital crime in golfing, it's the cynicism and dishonesty of so many resorts that claim they require carts because it speeds up play. Clearly, carts merely provide another assured income stream for golf courses that may already be charging $150 for a round. Carts actually *slow* play, and every purist should commit himself to driving at least one cart into a water hazard sometime very soon.

To me, the gravest, most unforgivable bastardization of the American game—proof that we've strayed almost irretrievably far from golf's true heart—is this dictatorship of the cart. This negates one of the very reasons that men began playing the game five centuries ago—to get some exercise in a lovely setting. It alienates us from the natural terrain, and probably keeps us from being better golfers because we don't have a feel for the land.

A sign on the first tee at North Berwick—no doubt installed to send a message to visitors from across the pond—reads: "A round of golf should not take more than three hours." (And that's on foot!) In the States, we've all played with guys who take that long just lining up their putts. Competing for a couple of dollars, a foursome of twenty handicaps will stand over their golf balls as if every stroke would determine the outcome of the Ryder Cup. Then they get testy when, after waiting behind them for an hour, you finally ask to play through.

"It's all backed up," they'll automatically lie, to preserve their own glacial pace, when the two holes in front of them are in fact clear.

Americans—who created the subculture of golf instruction, golf schools, golf videotapes, swing aids, high-tech clubs, and other highly self-conscious, analytical, antitranscendent approaches to the game—play slowly. Addressing my own ball, for instance, I've learned to work first on my grip—turn my right hand toward the top of the club, interlock my fingers, and remember to hold on loosely. I line up from behind the ball by identifying interim targets. I consider my stance, align my feet, square my shoulders, aim the club face, and visualize the shot. I think about swing plane, hip rotation, weight shift, how far back to take the club, moving from the inside out, and following through. I try to recall every word that every golf pro ever uttered to me. Then I remember the Zen lesson about letting go of all such subjective thoughts, and try to forget it all. No wonder we spend five hours playing eighteen holes.

The speed with which Scots seem to race across the terrain actually points out an essential philosophical difference from the American style of play, and demonstrates that the inventors of the game intuitively understand golf's transcendent heart. Of course, a Scot would never consciously identify and utter this understanding, because doing so would be antitranscendent. A Scottish golfer walks briskly up to his ball, peeks at the flag, grabs a club, and hits. Before the ball even lands, he's on his way again. Lacking yardage markers, he just feels which club is appropriate, and if it's the wrong choice, he doesn't whine about it for the next two holes. It might actually improve your game dramatically if you limited analysis of your golf swing to your practice time at the driving range, and simply played the game while you're out on the course. And you'd probably get home in time for dinner as well.

Scottish golfers play a sport entirely different from most Americans'. Theirs is a game of process, not product, a game where the journey itself matters most. They hardly worry about the end result—their score—unless they're engaged in a match. In fact, unless they're competing, they usually don't even keep score. (Don't try this at home; Americans are virtually incapable of not keeping score.) They play from the forward tees, with a total lack of bravado. They call a "Mulligan" a three.

• • •

But these are mostly rational reasons why Scottish golf expresses the game's true heart. Beyond logic, golfing in Scotland is inexplicably magical. I can only recommend driving up to Royal Dornoch or Turnberry or Royal Troon early on a cold October morning, when the chilly sea wind blows the flags ragged, light squeezes slowly out of the east, and the golf course spreads before you like the very edge of civilization—a healing place of mystery and possibility. When you arrive, the starter will have been expecting you, and he'll send you off the first tee with a quiet benediction, a few words of optimism and hope, the last words you'll hear before hitting out into that vast back country of the spirit, where the land is as wild and undiluted as it's always been, and you want only to blend into and become one with those natural aspects: green earth, clear water, translucent sky.

Back in the States, when I wish to reconnect to the ancient, beating heart of golf, I don't go play some manicured layout where the fairways are flat, predictable, lined with condos, and buzzing with motorized carts. Instead, I carefully—almost religiously—remove a bottle of twelve-year-old Scotch whisky from its secret hiding place and pour a measure of the amber liquid into a low crystal glass. I don't even care for the flavor all that much, but as the drink rolls across my tongue, I can smell burning peat beneath a gray sky, taste the salt air, envision the green links, and truly *feel* the buoyancy of connection, of Oneness, warming me all the way through.

CHAPTER TWO

Samurai Golf School

Flexibility is a primary consideration, and not just in the physical sense. The ability to adapt to circumstances psychologically and emotionally was crucial.
—*Commentary on Miyamoto Musashi's* The Book of Five Rings

The Head Pro was about to choose one of the assistant pros to help with lessons at the club. He called all of the assistant pros before him on the putting green late one afternoon, after all the members had gone home.

The Head Pro placed a pitcher of beer on the grass and posed this question: "If you cannot call it a beer pitcher, what do you call it?"

The seniormost assistant pro said, "It cannot be called a graphite driver."

The Head Pro then asked Guishan. Guishan immediately kicked over the pitcher and left.

The Head Pro smiled and said, "The
seniormost assistant pro has lost the tee." And
so he had Guishan begin teaching lessons the
next day.

—Zen golf koan

ONE OF MY CLOSEST FRIENDS (I CAN'T MENTION HIS NAME
because his wife would kill him if she knew this) has
been conducting a small experiment with their baby. The results probably won't be conclusive for another five or ten
years, but sometimes you have to be patient in the name of
science.

It's a very simple experiment, really. The baby has just
entered that stage where he eats a lot of fruit—he's absolutely
captivated by fruit—and when my friend is in charge of feed-
ing, every time he gives the baby a half of a peeled grape, he
whispers, "Apple!"

The point of the experiment, I think, is for my friend to
learn something about language and the perception of reality—
maybe to prove that whether we call a small, round, green,
seedless fruit an apple or a shark, its intrinsic grapeness, its
underlying reality, remains constant. Perceptions, whether accurate or not, are based on physical principles, not on language. Language simply helps us to communicate our
perceptions and check whether other humans are experiencing
something in the same way. When discussing unchanging principles that are not open to interpretation—that hot air rises,
or that the New York Jets won't win another Super Bowl—
we can employ language to ensure that we share a common
understanding of such fixed laws. But language also causes
some problems we must transcend, because words, as well as

22

our perceptions, necessarily carry subjective impressions and biases that cloud true reality.

The greatest challenge facing teachers, whether they're parents or professors, gurus or golf pros, is to establish a common language to talk about a complex principle, define its terms, and use that language to compare perceptions and ensure that everyone perceives the principle, or reality, in the same way. When I use the word *green,* for example, we must not only agree that green is a color, but we must also agree that it's the color of things such as grass and limes and many pairs of ugly golf pants. Simultaneously, however, great teachers must get beyond language to communicate the ultimate reality of experience. This challenge clearly reflects the Eastern concept of a reality beyond our intellectually biased perception of reality, and has applications far beyond esoteric spiritual teachings.

At an even more complex level, these are the challenges in teaching someone the golf swing—or at least in teaching it to me. While the task of defining terms such as *inside-out swing path* or *hand roll* may prove difficult in itself, ensuring that a student actually perceives and then applies such concepts correctly is a daunting task.

I recently spent two and a half days at the excellent Innisbrook Golf Institute, in Tarpon Springs, Florida, learning the fundamentals of a good golf swing, and discovering everything that was flawed in my own swing (a daunting undertaking). In some instances, the problems with my swing were based on bad information: Somebody had once told me that I was standing too far away from the ball, for example, so for the past ten years I've been crowding my setup, overcompensating for an earlier problem that doesn't exist anymore, if in fact it ever did. Some problems were based on a flawed understanding—such as thinking that I wasn't supposed to cock my wrists in the backswing. But in other instances, my *perceptions* of what I was doing in the swing were askew; I knew and understood the proper technique, but felt I was already accomplishing certain aspects of perfect form, when in fact I was behaving differently than I imagined, and mistakenly perceiving my actions as correct.

My swing path provides a perfect case study. On my first day at the Institute, instructor Dawn Mercer stood behind me watching my swing—which naturally deserted me the moment she began observing, so that I topped half a dozen balls thirty yards off the tee. Dawn wasn't much interested in my explanation of how well I usually hit a seven iron; when she couldn't bear to watch me duff one more shot, she approached with a can of spray paint, and I feared she was going to deface me as if I were a New York City subway car. Instead, she painted a sweeping white arc on the grass at my feet, labeled a spot behind me and to the right, at the back end of the arc, with the number seven, and a spot in front of me and to the right, at the start of the arc, with the number one. Then she explained that if the ball was positioned in the middle of a clock and I was straddling the nine o'clock position, the proper swing would travel on the arc between the six o'clock and twelve o'clock positions—six being exactly opposite my target, behind me, and twelve being the exact direction of my target, as well as the point of impact.

I've been pretty successful at telling time for the past few years of my life, so I said, "If my swing is supposed to travel between six and twelve, why did you draw seven and one on the ground? Do you want me to be late? Besides," I declared,

"I *am* swinging between six and twelve, at the target. I can feel it."

Dawn looked at me as if I'd just called a grape a shark.

"You *perceive* that you're swinging between six and twelve, but the reality is really more like five and eleven," she said. "Your perception is off, even though your actual swing is okay. In reality, you're swinging outside to inside, across your body. That causes you either to slice the ball or to overcompensate by hitting too far left. You won't actually be swinging at seven and one if you follow this path. You'll actually be on the six-twelve axis, but for you to do that, since your perception is off, you'll need to perceive as if you're swinging between seven and one."

Since Dawn's descriptions of slicing and hitting too far left characterized my range of golf shots fairly well, I stopped arguing. I nodded my head. I looked down at the clock. "What about the fact that cocktail hour often occurs between six and seven o'clock?" I asked.

Dawn moved on to help another student and left me trying to decide whether I really believed what she'd told me: in essence, that my perception of the world was slightly off and that this was getting in the way of my seeing reality clearly. Without her standing there peering over my shoulder, I murdered a long series of huge, towering seven irons, and thought, "*I* don't need golf school." I was pretty certain that I was swinging in a perfect line at my target. Even if I wasn't, I was hitting some great shots, with only the slightest hint of a fade. What more could a golfer want?

A few minutes later, Lew Smither III, Innisbrook's director of instruction, came over to watch me, and I topped half a dozen balls in *his* honor before he said, "Your swing path is moving outside in. You need to swing between six o'clock and twelve o'clock." Then he looked down at the white arc painted on the ground. "I see Dawn's already worked with you on this." I was more apt to believe Lew—not because he was a man, or because he was the director of instruction, or even because he was the second expert in ten minutes to tell me the same thing, but because I normally tend to believe people with Roman numerals in their names. They seem so rooted, so trustworthy.

Lew also offered insight concerning another perception problem in my golf swing. "You're very right-eye dominant," he observed, watching me line up and strike a few more balls. He couldn't possibly have known anything about my eyesight, which renders me unable to see an NFL linebacker standing directly in front of me if I'm using only my left eye.

"That may be part of what's causing your problem with swing path," Lew explained. "The way you stand over the ball, you see everything much more strongly with your right eye, from the right side, which tends to make you perceive 'straight' as being slightly off to the left. So your swing path moves around to eleven o'clock. If you cock your head back just a little—turn to the right the way Jack Nicklaus does after he's set up—then your left eye will be more involved in the shot, and you'll more accurately perceive the straight direction that you want to hit in." Lew then indicated my divot patterns on the ground, which all pointed incriminatingly left of the target area, proving his and Dawn's assertion.

As I practiced swinging the club in a direction that seemed way too far to the right of my target, I thought about having to redefine my perception of what was straight. I knew I tended to view most things in the world a little bit to the left (not only politically speaking), but I hadn't ever thought about my golf swing in those terms. So I recognized another hidden aspect of golf that had metaphorical implications beyond the game itself.

In a way, it was reassuring to hear that only my perception, and not my actual swing, was flawed. That seemed like an easier thing to correct. It wasn't until the second day at Innisbrook that they revealed to me just a few of the things that were wrong with my swing.

By the end of that next morning, when our instructors had stood over us at the practice range with stun guns for about thirty-five hours (and that was all before lunch), I began to realize how utterly complex a motion the golf swing is, and how difficult it must be to teach someone how to perform it well. I recognized how an overwhelmingly large number of interdependent motions must be executed correctly at the same time. And I understood how the biggest challenge of all was teaching students not only what constitutes correct form in regard to each of those separate motions, but also how to perceive and then copy those motions accurately when analyzing and trying to correct our own swings.

One component of the Innisbrook philosophy is that the golf swing depends on proper PGA—that is, posture, grip, and alignment. For readers who would like a very quick summary of a couple of the Institute's teachings (including advice regarding posture and grip), I'm including a few paragraphs from their teaching manual, which the Innisbrook staff was gracious enough to let me pass along. However, if you'd like to learn more, you'll have to sign up for a school.

The introduction to this book made quite a big deal about how these chapters would not really offer straight instructional materials, but would instead present some Eastern golf secrets. To that end, I've juxtaposed the instructional materials from Innisbrook with a few paragraphs taken from a great Eastern instructional book—Miyamoto Musashi's *The Book of Five Rings.* Musashi was a sixteenth-century samurai warrior, and I'll let his advice on swordsmanship speak for itself. Allow me just to point out that the term *iron,* which we now use to refer to most of the golf clubs in our bag, was once used by the Scots to refer to swords.

On Posture

The posture of your body influences the initial plane and path of your golf swing. Your body should be in an athletic position so that you are able to move in balance as you swing the golf club. The feet should be shoulder-width apart with the weight being balanced between the balls and heels and the knees slightly flexed.

Tilt the upper body forward at the hips to allow for a free arm swing around the body. Keep your head up and your eyes on the ball, which will allow the shoulders to turn more freely and help you to maintain visual contact with the ball.

—Innisbrook Golf Institute Teaching Manual

As for body posture, do not raise or lower the head or lean it to the side. Do not let the eyes wander. . . . From the shoulders down, maintain an even distribution of tension throughout the entire body. Lower both shoulders, hold the back straight, and do not stick out the buttocks. Tense the legs between the knees and the toes. . . .

—Miyamoto Musashi, The Book of Five Rings

ON GRIP

We recommend that you position the club diagonally across the first joint of the index finger and underneath the heel pad of the lead hand. Now place your trail hand below your lead hand so that the club rests more in the fingers than in the palm. . . . Positioning the hands on the club in this manner allows maximum feel and security. . . . The most effective way to keep tension out is to maintain light, even grip pressure throughout the swing.

—Innisbrook Golf Institute Teaching Manual

As for the manner of holding the long sword, hold it rather lightly with the thumb and index finger, neither firmly nor lightly with the middle finger, and firmly with the ring and little fingers. It is not good to have slackness in the hand. . . . In general, whether in long swords or in the manner of holding a sword, I dislike rigidity. Rigidity means a dead hand and flexibility means a living hand. One must understand this fully.

—Miyamoto Musashi, The Book of Five Rings

29

ON SPEED OF MOTION

This is not to say, "swing as hard as you can." You must find your optimum rate of speed, one in which you can swing, making solid contact and remaining in balance.

—Innisbrook Golf Institute Teaching Manual

Speed is not the true way. Speed is the fastness or the slowness which occurs when the rhythm is out of synchronization.

—*Miyamoto Musashi,* The Book of Five Rings

ON PRACTICE

A sound, repetitive pre-swing routine will assist you in your proper posture, grip, and alignment on a more consistent basis. . . . Establish and practice a mental and physical pre-swing routine and make this routine second nature. This gives you confidence, concentration, and composure even in the most pressure situations. . . . Once that particular position or movement becomes subconscious, it is automatic and repetitive, and all you have to do is let it happen.

—Innisbrook Golf Institute Teaching Manual

To practice whatever you do the same way all the time is a must. To practice a technique only half-heartedly builds bad habits, and lessens one's practice time of the proper technique. Remember that the context here is life and death swordplay, with razor-sharp, four-foot-long

lengths of steel. Remember also that dishonesty to one-
self was bad discipline.

—*Commentary on Miyamoto Musashi's* The Book of Five Rings

After pounding out three or four hundred thousand seven
irons on that second morning at the Institute, I looked up from
my station to gain some perspective on how my fellow students were faring and to see what kind of techniques our
instructors were using to communicate so much complex technical information. Two tees down from where I was hitting,
an older woman named Jeannie was practicing her short irons
while holding an orange ballon between her knees. Next to
her, Alexandra, who works for Innisbrook's marketing department, was imprisoned in a metal contraption intended to
prevent her from collapsing her inside arm during the backswing. Thirty yards behind them, Dieter, one of eight Germans in our class, was swinging what looked like a greatly
elongated cane for a very tall blind man around and around in
wide, dangerous arcs.

These swing aids provided a means—beyond the widely
subjective vagaries of language—of ensuring that we perceived
the correct motion of whatever aspect of the golf swing that
particular gadget was designed to teach. The balloon, for instance, allowed Jeannie to feel how her knees should remain
the same distance apart even as she shifted her weight during
the swing. When I was failing to rotate my hands over at the
point of contact (a motion that should feel like hitting a topspin
shot in tennis), Dawn handed me a sort of grotesque, disfig-
ured, bottom-heavy club that forced my hands over when I
swung it, so I couldn't possibly fail to perceive what correct
form should feel like. These aids cut through any subjective

31

perceptions we might have had and delivered a pure, clear dose of the experience of reality in much the same way that Zen Masters occasionally smacked their students with bamboo sticks to shock them out of their own subjectivism.

Just from watching our group for a few minutes, I determined that if you consider each of the myriad variables in the golf swing that must all happen correctly and simultaneously and then calculate the possibility of doing any of them wrong at any given time, there must be approximately 23,000 different possible mistakes. The opportunities for messing up are endless, and the chances of actually getting everything right at once seem very remote. But our instructors were unbelievably patient and almost good-natured about working through this tangled labyrinth one problem at a time.

Probably the most foolproof technique they employed to ensure proper perception of proper form was videotape, which allowed us to see what we were actually doing during our swings—incontestable reality!—as opposed to what we felt like we were doing. It's tough to argue with videotape, and in our class it produced a number of heartfelt "Ahas!"

Golf-swing videotapes work in much the same way as group psychotherapy. Let's say that you perceive that someone else in the group is angry with you. The best way to discover whether this perception is correct is to check it out objectively, from outside, by saying, "Are you angry with me?" If the person is angry, then he tells you so, reinforcing a correct perception and providing you with a chance to deal with the actual problem. And if you were wrong, and the person isn't angry with you at all, then you learn how your perceptions may differ from reality, and how you might fine-tune them to gain a more accurate view of the world.

Lew Smither filmed each of us on our first and second days at the Institute and carefully analyzed the tapes with us individually, until we truly understood what they revealed. The tapes provided an objective, outside view—unencumbered by the subjectivity of perception—of how we were really moving through our swings. On my own first-day tape, I can clearly see that I was swinging outside in, that my left shoulder dropped down too far, and that I began the downswing with my arms instead of my hips. On the second day's video, my swing was much cleaner; at the very end I executed a couple of nearly flawless swings, and Lew's last words on the tape were "Xerox that."

Anytime I worry about lapsing back into old patterns, I need only cozy up on the couch in my living room with a glass of wine (or Scotch) and the lights down low, and watch a graphic, intimate video of my own golf swing, complete with Lew's commentary about what I need to work on. Now if I could just find out whether Lew is angry with me.

> Begin with your short irons, then mid-irons, then the long irons. Next hit a few woods until you feel entirely warmed up. Hit all the shots. This means not only work on your swing, but hit the shot you will need in competition, i.e., fades, draws, bare lies, rough, high, low, recovery shots, etc.
>
> —Innisbrook Golf Institute Teaching Manual

> The warrior, in accordance with his aims, maintains various weapons and knows their characteristics and uses them well. This is the way of the warrior. Is it not an indication of superficial accomplishment of a warrior if

he does not master various weapons and understand individual weapons?

—*Miyamoto Musashi,* The Book of Five Rings

Of course, not all of our classroom time at the Institute
was spent slugging practice balls with a seven iron. We also
worked intensely on putting, chipping, pitching, and bunker
play, all taught by short-game expert Sue Knight. We
learned how to hit chip shots that run low, with minimum
air time and maximum roll. We learned how to pitch the
ball high to maximize air time and minimize roll. We
learned explosion shots, and how to knock a buried lie out
of the sand. We even practiced with our "long swords," or
drivers. And in the late afternoons, our brave instructors
dared to lead us out onto the golf course to play short
scrambles.

Since the majority of our class had not really golfed before, our instructors must have felt that venturing out on Innisbrook's Island course with us was not unlike taking a
bunch of children to a bar: Most of the group didn't really
know how to behave. So it was a good thing that this part
of the workshop included advice on etiquette, strategy, and
course management. Although I was by far the most experienced golfer in our class, I seemed to have acquired golf
amnesia when we got out on the links, and I managed to
mis-hit practically every shot I took. If you're an instructor,
about the only thing you can tell an experienced player who
continually shanks it into the woods is "Try not to continually shank it into the woods." I could see that our teachers
all felt bad for me, but not half as bad as I felt when Lew
knocked out a massive tee shot using the *back* of his driver.

Fortunately, just as we were finishing up on the practice range on our second day of instruction, some bad weather rolled in from the Gulf of Mexico. So instead of the golf course, we scrambled to the Sandpiper Bar, where I thought we all handled ourselves rather skillfully—the Germans in particular.

On our third and final morning, we reviewed the different shots we'd learned, practiced a little more, and then Lew, Dawn, and Sue presented each of us with our personalized videotapes and sent us off to pursue improved lives in golf. That afternoon, I had the unique experience of playing Innisbrook's famously difficult Copperhead course with my new German friend Sven, whom I convinced to join me even though he'd never played golf on an actual course before in his life. To guarantee that he'd have a memorable experience, I encouraged him to hit from the blue tees.

On the number-one tee, Sven knocked his first two shots into the woods. The advantage of his being such a novice player was that he didn't hit them very far, so they were easy to find. Whereas he'd been easygoing and calm on the practice range, developing a rather admirable swing in two and a half days, on the first tee at Copperhead he was visibly tense. I was tense as well, mostly because Sven was playing with rental clubs; since rental sets don't come with golf balls, I was supplying him. And there was plenty of water over the next eighteen holes.

But after a short while, Sven began hitting some admirable long-iron shots and playing well around the greens. The Institute had worked wonders with his game, and you couldn't have distinguished him from many golfers who claim to have twenty handicaps, except that he was wearing pink slacks and red tennis shoes, sported several silver Indian bracelets, and had his hair tied back in a ponytail. Sven was exhilarated by his play; while he'd easily gotten tired and bored after relentless hours of smacking range balls, out on the course he suddenly loved the game. He tried to think of ways he could manage to play back home in Germany. He wondered how much a set of clubs might cost.

Then he had a bad hole. He topped six shots and knocked another one in the water. He hated golf. It was stupid. He never wanted to play again.

I was amazed that in such a short time Sven had already mastered the entire range of golf emotions, and I reflected that his subsequent career would consist merely of endless variations of the euphoria and disgust he'd already experienced by the fourth hole.

Somehow Sven lost only three golf balls on Copperhead, and as we rode back up from the eighteenth green toward the clubhouse bar—where he could expect to excel—I think he actually believed that golf could be fun. I was less certain. I'd had a forgettable round, which included some great shots as well as a few I'd rather not talk about. But Lew had warned us not to expect much improvement in the short term—in fact, to expect regression—until we'd had ample time to practice all that we'd just learned.

For me, those three days at Innisbrook proved extremely valuable, and not just in terms of telling time. In addition to learning so many particulars about my own golf swing, and how correct form should actually look and feel, I also learned a few essential lessons about how I view the world—and that keeping my perceptions flexible and adaptable is the most important part of learning anything, on or off the fairway.

Each student learns how and why things happen in their particular golf swings. . . . You, by yourself, can develop your golf swing. . . . There is a right swing for each individual and when that is learned and developed, it becomes automatic and repetitive.

—Innisbrook Golf Institute Teaching Manual

Do not allow the words to hold back your understanding. As words, they are inadequate. . . . Remember that this is to be your own experience. Let the words point you in a direction: you make the trip yourself. Open your mind to all possibilities. When you read "long sword," do not let your mind stop at "long sword." For Musashi, the tool was a shining steel blade. For a painter, it is the brush and the paint. For a lawyer, it is words, for a truck driver it is the truck and its schedule, and for the person in business it is the negotiating and arranging of events that makes one successful. Let your creative mind understand, deeply and intuitively.

—*Commentary on Miyamoto Musashi's* The Book of Five Rings

CHAPTER THREE

Under the Covers: An Intimate Look at the Secret Life of Golf Balls

The flute without the holes is the most difficult to blow.

—from Toyo Eicho Zenji's sixteenth-century compilation,
A Phrase Book

The Zen philosopher Basho once wrote, "A flute with no holes is not a flute, and a doughnut with no hole is a danish. . . . Na na na na na na na na na . . ."

—Chevy Chase in the Zen golf movie Caddyshack

L ET'S SAY THAT YOU'RE STANDING ON THE ELEVATED TEE OF
one of the most difficult holes on a golf course that you play
often: it's a long, narrow par four with OB to the right and water encroaching upon the fairway from the left and running all
the way up to the green. Since you've been known in your lifetime to slice a drive every now and again, you set up by aiming
left of the fairway, at about ten o'clock at the blue corner of the
lake, so that when your ball inevitably tails off it will curl away
from the water and kick right into the garden spot at noon.

But for some unfathomable reason, just as you finish your
pre-shot routine, plant your feet, and draw the club back,
every element of your swing finally, and for the first time
ever, falls perfectly into place—an occurrence that ruins your
tee shot because you've adjusted your entire game to compensate for slicing. Your downswing is flawless. You launch a
long, immaculately straight drive that never wavers from its
direct course and goes precisely where you aimed it. The ball
splashes thirty yards out into the drink.

"Nice shot," says your best friend, playing companion, and
archrival, shaking his head ruefully, feigning commiseration, as
if he's deeply sorry that such a well-struck ball should cost
you a penalty stroke. A few moments later, though, you shut
him up by dropping another ball next to the hazard and punch-
ing it onto the green with a three iron. Then you drain a long
putt to win the hole with a par.

Later this afternoon, recounting your round from the lounge
chair in the yard as you sip iced tea and drift off toward the
fluffy border of napland, you'll probably meditate upon this
excellent recovery. Still, chances are that you'll never give
another thought to that brand-new golf ball you knocked into
the lake.

Which is a shame, because when viewed from beyond the ordinary perspective of the fairway, a golf ball—possibly the most integral yet undervalued item of essential equipment in the sport—can teach you a great many lessons. By altering your normal perception of golf balls, and looking at them with a fresh eye, you can learn about such disciplines as history, physics, engineering, philosophy, and even physical education (every curriculum needs a gut course), and apply your new-found understanding of these subjects to deepen your enjoyment and appreciation of the game. Not to mention impressing your friends and neighbors with the breadth of your education.

HISTORY

Contrary to its simple, unobtrusive appearance when sitting cozily up on the manicured grass of the fairway, the golf ball is actually a highly evolved product of technologies that have improved it dramatically over the past five centuries. And all these innovations began with an *aha!* moment or a revelation in which somebody suddenly perceived the golf ball in a new way.

As early as the 1400s, royal ball makers in Britain produced some of the first golf balls—called featheries—by stuffing a top hat full of feathers into a wet leather pouch and then waiting for the leather to dry and shrink. A skilled craftsman could create four of the balls in a day. Featheries exerted an autocratic influence over golf for several centuries, until a British missionary visiting Malaysia in the 1800s discovered a thick, sticky substance seeping out of a local gutta-percha tree. He brought a sample of the substance back to

Britain, and a short time later a man named Bob Patterson, of St. Andrews, Scotland, began shaping gutta-percha rubber into golf balls. Patterson's motivation was purely selfish: He could not afford to buy expensive featheries. But his new ball proved to have more than just economic benefits. Gutties also traveled farther and were more durable in wet weather than featheries, which grew soggy. The major drawback of the new ball was its tendency to split into pieces. In such cases, local rules generally required golfers to play the largest piece. However, in the great Scottish tradition of economizing, you could always take a broken gutty home at the end of the day and patch it back together.

As the industrial revolution changed the character and pace of much of the civilized world toward the end of the nineteenth century, Coburn Haskell sparked a similar revolution in golf ball technology. In 1898, Haskell invented a ball with a rubber core that he hand-wound with elastic thread (he was already in the garter and suspender business) before covering. The ball traveled twenty to fifty yards farther than the gutty. When Walter Travis won the U.S. Amateur with a Haskell in 1901, and Sandy Herd won the British Open with the ball the following year, it signaled the end of the gutta-percha's reign of power.

For a number of years already, golfers had recognized that for some reason scratched or scuffed balls seemed to fly truer than smooth ones. It was common practice for golfers to roughen their own golf balls with all sorts of gouges and cuts before teeing them up. In 1908, John Taylor sparked the next major insurrection in golf ball history when he received a patent for golf ball dimples. Until then, many balls were manufactured with brambles, or raised dots, but Taylor's new design proved that balls with dimples traveled farther and straighter than even randomly gouged balls. A year later, the Spalding Company began manufacturing the Glory golf ball, which featured uniform dimples on its cover. Glories sold for nine dollars per dozen, the equivalent of about $300 today—which may explain why golf was played mostly by wealthy capitalists early in the century.

By the 1920s—an era characterized by flappers and bootleg whiskey—anarchy reigned in the golf ball industry as well. Various companies were manufacturing hundreds of types and varieties of balls. In an effort to impose a modicum of order on the sport, the USGA asserted its own political clout by instituting strict specifications for characteristics such as the size and weight of golf balls. Many of these laws still govern the game today.

As the twentieth century progressed, golf ball manufacturers developed synthetic materials that matched the properties of such natural but expensive substances as balata rubber. Most companies also abandoned one- and three-piece designs in favor of two-piece balls consisting of a solid core with a separate plastic cover. Although the history of the golf ball stabilized during this period, a dramatic upheaval did affect one seemingly innocuous but truly essential component of the ball. In 1973, William Gobush, of the Titleist Company, received a patent for a new golf ball dimple pattern consisting of twenty triangles, called an icosahedron, which allowed manufacturers to cover a greater area of the ball's surface with dimples (see the "Physics" section for an explanation of dimples). Until that time, dimples could only cover approximately 65 percent of a ball, but Gobush's new design allowed for up to 73 percent coverage. Ten years later, he achieved another breakthrough: By employing a sort of two-party system of larger and smaller dimples, he mananged to cover 78 percent of a ball. And more recently, by using an even more democratic variety of dimple sizes, Gobush achieved coverage as high as 83 percent.

Over the past few years, the unrest that characterized the earlier days in golf ball history has faded to a distant memory. Recent changes in golf balls have represented modifications (such as in color, feel, and trajectory) rather than revolutions. Perhaps the most innovative change of the decade was Spalding's creation of the Top-Flite Magna—a slightly oversized ball designed for less-skilled players, which achieves greater distance at slower swing speeds than any other ball.

However, don't misconstrue the slowdown in golf ball evolution as a sign of complacency. Researchers are currently experimenting with new materials, designs, and processes in an effort to see the golf ball in new ways and to create balls that may eventually satisfy every golf constituency—from hookers to slicers to older players with less strength. Even so, history may pass by apathetic golfers with lousy swings unless they become more actively involved in improving their own fundamentals.

PHYSICS

Physics is—among other things—an attempt to harmonize with a much greater entity than ourselves, requiring us to seek, formulate, and eradicate first one and then another of our most cherished prejudices and oldest habits of thought, in a never-ending quest for the unattainable.

—*David Finkelstein, in the foreword to Gary Zukav's*
The Dancing Wu Li Masters

To reach a true and deep understanding of the golf ball, you must penetrate beyond the ball's appearance and learn about the scientific principles, the true reality that makes it behave the way it does. For my own personal tutorial on this subject, I consulted Joseph Stiefel, the Spalding Company's resident physicist, whose office looks a lot like my sports closet at home—littered with basketballs, footballs, tennis rackets, golf clubs, and other athletic gear. While visiting Spalding's offices and factory in Chicopee, Massachusetts, I had the hardest time refraining from dribbling, shooting, or swinging some piece of equipment in the hallways, and I wondered how employees ever get any work done. If I took a job there, I'd constantly be kicking soccer balls at the narrow doorways of other people's offices, or executing hook shots over the top of my cubicle to test my colleagues' reflexes.

After I found a bleacher seat near his desk, Stiefel provided me with a crash course in physics to explain how various components of the golf ball—particularly its core composition, cover composition, and the size, pattern, depth, and shape of surface dimples—affect its spin, durability, distance, trajectory, and feel.

He began by explaining that the amount a golf ball spins depends upon the softness of its cover. Soft-covered balls spin more because upon contact, the club face sticks to the cover longer than it does against a harder-covered ball, which tends to slip up the face of the club. Longer contact translates to more spin because the club spends more time pushing against the ball. Added spin makes the ball more workable for a good player—or more likely to be hit into the woods by a less-skilled player, who may spin it sideways. The hardness or softness of the cover depends upon its chemical composition, but since chemistry is not part of this curriculum, I didn't pursue the subject any further. Spalding makes covers of at least four different levels of hardness.

Still, nothing in physics is quite as simple as it first sounds. When you strike a ball with a club such as a low iron or a wood—clubs that you normally swing with more force than you'd employ when swinging a wedge, for example—the ball's core composition also affects its spin. A soft core gives more, absorbing some of the impact that would otherwise be transformed into increased spin if you were hitting a harder-core ball with a longer club. Therefore, balls with hard cores under soft covers will spin the most, and those with hard covers over soft cores will spin the least.

A golf ball's cover also determines its durability, which seemed rather obvious even to me. Soft-covered balls are more likely to cut upon contact, and require replacing. However, since hard-covered balls spin less, and are therefore easier to control, they're most often played by less-skilled players, who are more likely to lose them, anyway—which seems to make the durability question a wash.

The distance a golf ball travels is also related to its core composition, in addition to depending upon whether John Daly or your sister is hitting it. The harder the core, the less impact it will absorb and the farther it will fly (or skid, depending on how you hit it). The hardness and compression of a solid core is determined by its chemistry—i.e., the type and amount of specific ingredients used; in wound cores, hardness is a function of how tightly the rubber thread composing the core is wrapped.

Golf ball companies currently possess the technology to produce balls that would regularly travel 300 yards or more when struck well. However, the USGA has imposed a limit of 280 yards in carry and roll for balls tested on the outdoor range at USGA headquarters, when hit by their approved ball machine at swing speeds of 160 mph. Golfers swinging faster than 160 mph may still hit the ball farther than 280 yards (if they can even make contact at such speeds), but the USGA will not approve any ball that exceeds these limits at 160 mph. Faced with this strict limitation, researchers have turned their attention to achieving other gains in regard to distance. For example, they have developed balls with softer cores and softer covers that provide maximum distance, but also offer other advantages, such as a soft feel and higher spin rates.

Distance is also determined to a lesser degree by a golf ball's dimples, which simultaneously exert almost complete control over the ball's trajectory. Whereas a perfectly smooth golf ball would take off normally from the clubhead at impact, about 150 yards away it would drop rather suddenly to the ground. By dimpling the surface of the ball, however, researchers can add an additional hundred yards or so of flight. While the ball is in motion, dimples grab the air around it, creating turbulence. Because air flows faster over the top of the ball than over the bottom as it spins, the ball rises. In general, larger, shallower dimples provide greater distance by maximizing lift, or trajectory. Physicists have spent many hours figuring out how to create low-trajectory balls that still achieve maximum distance (they use fewer dimples and a slightly harder core). They have also struggled to design better balls under the manufacturing constraint that dimples cannot cross the equator of the ball, because no existing machine could trim the hangnails of cover flashing (which sometimes appear on the equator during manufacturing) out of the recessed dimples. (See the next section, "Engineering," for a more in-depth explanation of flashing.)

When Joseph Stiefel came to work for Spalding in 1986, scientists in his office created new dimple patterns by pasting white paper shapes on a bowling ball—a labor-intensive process. Currently, with the help of computer-aided design, they can now invent experimental patterns in minutes, and transform these models into molds to produce actual test balls in two or three weeks. During his own tenure, Stiefel has tested more than 150 dimple patterns. Although most have employed pure mathematical layouts such as the icosahedron, he's also tried what he calls "some wacky patterns." Apparently physicists dream about new golf ball dimple designs in much the same way I dream about dramatically beating Greg Norman to win a major. One Spalding scientist even received inspiration for a new design while staring at an ear of corn in his garden.

ENGINEERING

My engineering lesson included a field visit to Spalding's golf ball factory, which churns out more balls in a single minute than the average golfer might lose in several lifetimes of

mediocre play. Mike Sullivan, Spalding's director of re-
search—also known fondly as the Ball Doctor—led me on the
grand tour. Although Sullivan looks suspiciously young enough
to be the Ball Medical Student, his knowledge of golf ball
mechanics and the concurrent engineering necessary to man-
ufacture a variety of performance balls is as dizzying as the
endless river of Top-Flites and Tour Editions pouring out of
the factory. The facility itself, called the Factory of the Future
by Spalding employees, houses state-of-the-art equipment in a
series of buildings that gives the feel of a well-maintained community college.

In a hulking corrugated structure down the street from the
actual factory, Spalding chemists mix various grades of synthetic rubber possessing different physical properties into slugs,
which look like large wads of blue bubble gum. Workers trans-
fer the slugs to the factory and load them by hand into individual molds—the last time humans will touch the balls until
they're ready for shipping. Once the slugs are happily encased
in their molds, compressing machines apply different levels of
heat and pressure to squeeze the slugs into smooth, round ball
cores in several different compressions and sizes. The cores—
which look like solid Ping-Pong balls—then enjoy an overhead
ride along a sort of monorail, which drops them into another
machine that brushes and tumbles the spheres to clean them
and remove any flashing—the rubber hairs sometimes formed
where the two pieces of the pressurizing mold fit together.
The cores then receive a soothing bath to shrink and cool
them. As they emerge, a worker removes impaired cores and
tosses them into one of three bins: blips, which are made into
cheap, generic golf balls; scraps, which are recycled into new
cores; and X-outs, which Spalding sells as cosmetically imper-

fect balls with the Top-Flite brand name barely legible under black *x*'s.

Cores passing the blip/scrap/X-out inspection travel in crowded leisure class to the injection molding department in the main room of the factory, which is as clean as a suburban rec room, climate-controlled to a crisp Scottish autumn temperature, and full of colorful machinery run by robots. The robots gently place the cores into dimpled molds and then inject synthetic cover material around them under high pressure, forming a protective outer shell similar to the colored candy coating that surrounds the chocolate in an M&M. Spalding uses fifteen or more different cover formulations to encase twelve or more different core formulations to create balls with different playing characteristics. Each machine can be set to create any of the variables, depending upon which ball is being manufactured at a given moment.

Once they've been formally dressed, the balls hitch a ride to the auto-milling department, where air pressure bounces them into position so that a spinning blade can trim the flashing from where the covers were injected. A laser examines the trimmed balls and rejects any that aren't militarily precise. Balls are then brushed and washed again to shake loose any flashing, and air-dried.

In the final factory process, four spray guns fire a priming coat at the balls as they spin past. When the priming dries, the balls samba down to a printing machine, which stamps them with logos before more guns shoot an armorlike coating of abrasion-resistant protection over the surface. The balls then cure for three to four hours in an oven before humans pick them up, wheel them into the packaging room, and load them into a last machine, which herds them into properly labeled boxes. Spalding ships these out to distributors, who in turn send them to retail outlets such as the pro shop at your local golf course.

PHYSICAL EDUCATION

Just as you needn't know anything about motorcycle maintenance to ride a Harley, Mike Sullivan suggests that many golfers needn't comprehend a single principle of physics or engineering to make excellent use of these bodies of knowledge and successfully drive a golf ball. All you need to do is figure out which golf ball is most appropriate for the way you play.

First, Sullivan recommends that players accurately characterize their own playing styles and then find a ball that best matches their needs. If you're a five handicap, for example, you can probably control the high spin of a soft-covered, hard-cored balata-type ball. If you're a hacker, the Top-Flite Magna (which Sullivan's group invented) may suit you best by offering less spin but still providing maximum distance at slower swing speeds. If cost is a major factor, you might simply choose the cheapest ball you can find—probably one with the logo of an oil company or tractor manufacturer—which has been gathering dust in the "experienced" bin in some pro shop for several years; Sullivan, however, who is somewhat partial, recommends you purchase Top-Flite XLs in the fifteen-ball value pack.

Sullivan also advises golfers to consider using different trajectory balls under different playing conditions. In high winds, for example, like those at Scottish links such as Carnoustie or

Royal Troon, or on a dry, flat course, choose a low-trajectory ball that will maximize roll. On a course with elevated greens ringed by hazards, a high-trajectory ball may keep you out of trouble.

Of course, the better you are as a player, the bigger the payoff will be for choosing the right ball. If you're going to hook it into the woods anyway, it won't matter if you tee up a grapefruit.

PHILOSOPHY

> The Buddha, the Godhead, resides quite as comfortably in the circuits of a digital computer or the gears of a cycle transmission as he does at the top of a mountain or in the petals of a flower.
> —*Robert Pirsig,* Zen and the Art of Motorcycle Maintenance

It is truly remarkable that in our travels through this world we don't stumble upon golf balls everywhere we go, that we don't find them drifted ten or twelve feet deep like windblown snow in the streets, or see them rolling by the thousands across open fields, or discover acres of them washed up on beaches at the edges of the Earth's continents. In 1992 alone, the Spalding Company manufactured twenty million dozen golf balls at its two factories in Massachusetts and New York—and that's just a single company in one year. It's safe to estimate the total number of golf balls out there in the world at *billions,* and it's an exercise in philosophy to consider where they all could possibly have gone.

For another thing, the average golf ball does not survive

51

even a single round of eighteen holes with its original owner. If we were somehow able to track the life experiences and various reincarnations of a particular ball as it disappears into woods and water holes and tall grass, as it's retrieved and resold and transported from course to course across state and even national borders in the pockets of golf bags, this view from beyond the fairway would suggest that just as Buddhists believe souls continually return to this world until they evolve toward enlightenment, golf balls also live many and varied lives.

Golf balls also provide a philosophical lesson in how we're all interrelated. By constantly changing hands, they create an invisible matrix that bridges the gaps of age, sex, nationality, economic class, and other factors that work to alienate and divide us. By closely considering the golf ball, we may catch a glimpse of each other in its reflection, and recognize that across this great planet with its teeming population, we're separated from one another by only a few poorly hit shots.

Take a moment to consider what might have happened to that shiny new ball that you knocked into the pond at the beginning of this chapter. Chances are that your club hires someone to dredge the water hazards for golf balls a few times each year. The pro may resell the best of these in his shop, and ship the rest off for resale somewhere else. (Of course, the guy who pulled the balls out of the water may also sell a few out of the trunk of his car in the parking lot of a nearby municipal course.) It's entirely possible that some morning, perusing the merchandise in the pro shop before your tee time, you might actually repurchase the very same ball that you already paid two bucks for when it was part of a new sleeve, and which you shortly thereafter knocked into the drink. This time, you may buy it for the bargain price of one dollar, without ever realizing what a happy reunion it is—though not necessarily for the ball, which may not harbor the fondest memories of you. With a little luck, however, the ball might fall to the bottom of your bag, ensuring a longer and more comfortable tenure.

Maybe you won't reach that far down into your bag for the rest of the season, and the ball will remain safe as the weather turns cold and your golf bag sits in the basement until, in April, you decide to take that trip to Pinehurst, and on the fifteenth hole of the Number Two course, after playing the same ball for nearly your entire round, you slice it into the woods, and search for it only halfheartedly because you're playing two-man best ball and your partner has cranked his tee shot into perfect position. So a youngster whose parents own a condo nearby finds your ball—covered with a bit of pine sap from its altercation with a tree—and takes it home to his father, who loses it the very next day on another hole, where an elderly ophthalmologist from Michigan comes across it in the deep grass and plays it from there, either pretending it's his own ball or simply not realizing that it isn't, and since he doesn't hit very far anymore, he manages to hold on to it for the rest of the round.

Perhaps he takes the ball home with him to the small town of Haslett, where it sits in his golf bag in the attic until his daughter, visiting from Palm Springs the following summer, carries the clubs out into the yard to hit some chip shots, but loses a couple of balls—including the one that was once *your* ball—over the fence in the fading light. A neighbor kid picks up the ball and stows it in his sock drawer until his family holds a yard sale, where a bookstore owner from Detroit, who'd been hoping to find an antique dresser, buys a dozen worn balls for two dollars, along with an ugly lamp made from an old rifle.

The bookstore owner gives the balls to her son just before his trip to Florida, where he loses all of them in the water hazards at Doral, where a scuba diver retrieves balls twice a year and sends yours to the pro shop—a destination with which it's becoming familiar. A nearsighted accountant from New York City buys the ball and eventually takes it to the Caribbean, where he hooks it into the ocean, from where it's retrieved by an island boy who sells it for a quarter to a college student on vacation with his parents.

By now, having absorbed several hundred blows, having been lost a dozen times, and having traveled thousands of miles, the ball has lost its abrasion-protective coating and exhibits a few scars. The student stores it in his bag for a while before ultimately losing it on a public course in Japan, where he's gone to teach English. Once it's found again, the ball is sold with thousands of others to a three-tiered driving range, and eventually sold again to a cruise company. On an overcast day in June, a cruise passenger hits it from the deck of a ship far out into the Mediterranean, where it finally sinks to the bottom alongside the ruins of a galleon that's lain on the sandy sea floor for centuries, waiting to be discovered by some treasure hunter who will marvel at how in the world this twentieth-century artifact came to lie beside riches from a much earlier epoch in history. Perhaps he'll even wonder about the crude materials and design of the ball.

All of which points out how the golf ball manages to connect and unite so many diverse and disparate people in the infinite Oneness. Next time you knock a ball into the lake encroaching upon the left side of the fairway on that squirrelly par four at your local golf course, look beyond the surface for the hidden implications of the event before simply pulling another ball out of your bag and hitting it toward the green.

PART TWO

On the Fringe:
Transcendence and
Visualization

———

CHAPTER FOUR

Artless Art, the Great Doctrine, and the Toughest Par-Three Course in the World

The "Great Doctrine" of archery tell us . . . that archery is still a matter of life and death to the extent that it is a contest of the archer with himself; and this kind of contest is not a paltry substitute, but the foundation of all contests outwardly directed—for instance with a bodily opponent. In this contest of the archer with himself is revealed the secret essence of this art. . . .

Anyone who subscribes to this art today, therefore, will gain from its historical development the undeniable advantage of not

being tempted to obscure his understanding of the
"Great Doctrine" by practical aims. . . . For
access to the art—and the master archers of all
times are agreed in this—is only granted to those
who are "pure" in heart, untroubled by
subsidiary aims.

—*Eugen Herrigel,* Zen in the Art of Archery

A new assistant pro asked the Head Pro, "I have
just come on staff and I request your
instruction."
   The Head Pro inquired, "Have you had your
morning coffee yet?"
   The new assistant pro said, "I have had my
coffee."
   The Head Pro said, "Then go wash your coffee
mug."
   That assistant pro had an insight.

—*Zen golf koan*

I THINK IT'S SAFE TO SAY THAT IF MY FRIEND CHARLIE BLAN-
chette and I were confined to wheelchairs in an old-age
home together, we'd probably wager our beer money on who
could roll to the music therapy class faster.

If my friend Jeff Wuorio also lived in the same home, he
wouldn't worry so much about beating Charlie and me to the
music room; he'd fret over traveling there as quickly and ef-
ficiently as he could possibly propel himself, and he wouldn't
make allowances for crashing into walls or dodging a nurse. If
Jeff didn't arrive in record time, setting a new personal best,
he'd be angry and disappointed with himself.

Which is another way of saying that my friends and I occasionally succumb to practical, subsidiary aims such as trying
to beat the heck out of each other in some kind of competition.

When competing against my friends, I'm unconcerned with using the game to change our relationship; I simply want to win, because beating them means something altogether different.

Nearly every golfer who's ever listened to even remotely noncompetitive theories about golf—for example, that it's just a game; that you should relax and enjoy yourself and forget about that quintuple bogey; that a bad day golfing is better than a good day working; that score doesn't matter; and that everyone is entitled to an off day—recognizes these as lies. Most folks who care about golf believe that each shot reflects their inner worth, their moral character, their power and position in the world. They know that golf is God's way of evaluating them as people, and of communicating that evaluation in a divine manner for all to see. Which is why it seems so unbelievably important not only to play the game well, but to win. Otherwise, you might have to face the inevitable truth that God likes your opponent better than He likes you.

Yet while a golf match is the essence of competition, in golf we play within ourselves as much as or more than in any other sport. No opponent pitches, serves, slaps, or kicks a ball toward us. No goalie defends against our efforts. Regardless of whether the wind is blowing or a particular shot requires a high loft to clear a hazard, the game's essential motion and rhythm remain the same.

What's more, most of us who've played the game have also discovered our own capability to hit near-perfect shots on occasion. We've learned that we possess at least the physical skills necessary to excel, unlike in baseball, for example, where our wrist speed wouldn't be adequate to knock a fastball over the center field fence, or in tennis, where we'd lack the power to serve at ninety miles per hour. Knowing that we can hit the right shot—just one among a wide spectrum of right shots—also relocates the game from the body to the mind. So, in addition to being a game that pits us against others, golf ultimately provides an inner competition in which we play ruthlessly against ourselves.

But striking a fine, balanced golf shot—or linking a series of them together into a great round—requires emptying the mind of conscious considerations such as beating an opponent or shooting a 75. It requires journeying to a place where nothing exists outside of golfer, golf club, and golf ball, and where the distinctions between these elements disappear, too. Some players call this "playing in the zone." Eastern philosophers might refer to it as transcendence.

All of this combines to present a baffling paradox, a mystical golf koan: Sports are by their very nature competitive. Golf, although a sport and therefore intrinsically competitive (both on personal and interpersonal levels), is also a Zen-like and transcendent sport. Zen by its very nature is noncompetitive, and considers goals such as winning or setting a new personal best to be practical, subsidiary aims that completely miss the point of the activity.

However, revelation often emerges from paradox, though such a transformation often calls for a change in perception.

One Sunday in June, my friends Jeff and Charlie and I played a skins game on the Lakeview Challenge golf course in Vancouver, Washington. Billed as the toughest par-three lay-out in the world, Lakeview provided the perfect location in which to consider the essence of competition, both internal and external; investigate our unenlightened emphasis on victory; examine transcendence and other new visions of the game; and maybe win a few bucks at the same time.

The Lakeview Challenge golf course was originally designed and built by a maniacal asphalt paving contractor—aptly named Duke Wager—for the dual purposes of (1) hosting private, highly competitive money games among several dozen of his closest friends (many of whom were low handicappers or local pros) and (2) vastly improving his own short game so he could win highly competitive money games among several dozen of his closest friends. In Zen, these would not constitute worthy spiritual goals, but in Washington State they seemed to work fine. Duke wasn't after enlightenment.

A thirteen handicap himself, Wager realized that to make his private contests more equitable and give himself a better chance of banking a few dollars, he might have to trick up the course a bit and create a layout difficult enough to neutralize a good player's advantages. He constructed ten bizarre holes— all except two of which are played twice—with unlikely greens, tees, and fairways on ten acres in an orchard behind his home (the greens fee covers all the apples, pears, plums, and walnuts you can eat). These holes not only pit players against each other in a perfectly adversarial, even hostile manner, but also set players against the course itself. Lakeview Challenge carries the notion of competitive golf to a new level, turning up the heat until some players simply boil over; as a reminder that this isn't simply another pitch-and-putt course, over time Duke has collected and displayed dozens of bent, broken, mangled, and abandoned golf clubs that he retrieved from the course's woods and water hazards.

When Duke opened the course to the public in the early 1980s, the scorecard contained several local rules that hinted at what the Lakeview experience might be like. These included a seven-stroke limit per hole, and such warnings as: "Do whatever is necessary to keep up with the group ahead of you," "No chip shots from the greens," and "No swimming or wading in the water hazards." For anyone who's seen the water hazards—which emit a green, toxic-looking glow—this last warning was totally unnecessary.

In the years that Wager managed the course, the lowest score ever recorded on the par-54, 1,900-yard layout was a 56, or two over par. He felt so confident that no golfer would ever shoot par that he offered $1,000 to anyone who could do so on a day when he set the pins in their most difficult positions.

Wager can talk for hours about course conditions in the good old days, when he still ran Lakeview as a private enclave for invited guests and you could lose a golf ball in the rough two feet from the green. He likes to explain how, on any given day, if he received phone calls from neighbors a block or two away complaining about the bad language emanating from the course, he knew the layout wasn't playing tough enough. If he heard from neighbors who lived five or six blocks away, he'd achieved the perfect level of difficulty and competitiveness.

So just how tough is tough? Wager describes a match that he was winning by 13 strokes going into the final hole, but he took a double-digit score and lost by one. The hole was only eighty yards long. "I was sick for days," he remembers. He also loves to tell about a two handicap who picked up a 38 on the seventy-nine-yard ninth. "His face was chalk white, his shirt was soaked with sweat, the poor bastard was on the verge of tears. It was great.''

Three years ago, Duke—who devoted much of his life to not manicuring the golf course, so that it remained nearly impossible—sold out to a far more practical and conservative man. Current owner Doug Greene trimmed the eight-inch rough on the fringes, slowed the greens from their 12+ on the Stimpmeter, and otherwise groomed Lakeview to play easier, which means it's now only marginally impossible. However, it's still tough enough that the modern (i.e., post-Wager) scoring record stands at 53, or one under par. Even while Greene curbed some of Lakeview Challenge's bite to make it more palatable to the fee-paying public, many holes still exhibit unpredictable, aberrant behavior. And the course retains an almost magical ability to transform calm, laid-back northwesterners into the fiercest Type A players. The kind of competitive golf it inspires is so far removed from the transcendent Zen nature of the game that it's the perfect backdrop against which to examine this paradox.

[The Zen swordsman] must be taught to be detached not only from his opponent but from himself. He must pass through the stage he is still at and leave it behind him for good, even at the risk of irretrievable failure. Does not this sound as nonsensical as the demand that the archer should hit without taking aim, that he should completely lose sight of the goal and his intention to hit it? It is worth remembering, however, that the master swordsman . . . has vindicated [himself] in a thousand contests.

—*Eugen Herrigel*, Zen in the Art of Archery

On the day that my friends and I staged our own modest competition at Lakeview Challenge, a sign in the parking lot read: "On a scale of 1 to 10, 10 being the most difficult, today is a 7." Beneath these words the sign displayed an illustration of an irate golfer breaking a club over his knee. The numbers referred to pin placements, and that they could vary so widely immediately implied that things would be different here. I also discovered from the greenskeeper that the day's pin placements *averaged* a 7, which meant that on the front they measured a moderate 5–6, but on the back (each green that you played twice had two pins) they were set at a misanthropic 9–10.

After Charlie and Jeff and I agreed to the specific terms of our contest—a skins game with carryovers, and bonus money won for pars and birdies—we teed off on the ninety-three-yard opener. The hole seemed unremarkable, and in no way prepared us for what was to come. The tee box consisted of a concrete slab overlaid with a square of Astroturf sprouting a driving-range tee. Judging by the way our golf balls bounced, the greens weren't much more welcoming.

I managed to bump and run my tee shot onto a distant edge of the sloping green, and then rolled in a forty-foot side-hill, banana-arced putt for birdie, which set the tone for the match. Jeff and Charlie were not amused. Walking toward the second tee a few moments later, we noticed a trap behind the first green that looked a lot like a freshly dug grave—our first indication of what we were in for. Jeff peered over the edge, then back at me, shaking his head. "Jesus Christ," he said, "they should have a chairlift for getting out of there."

[Master:] The more obstinately you try to shoot the arrow for the sake of hitting the goal, the less you will succeed in the one and the further the other will recede.
———*Eugen Herrigel,* Zen in the Art of Archery

Lakeview Challenge began to express its mean-spirited personality on the second hole, a 128-yarder with a tall pine tree in the middle of the narrow fairway, halfway to the green. To prevent wimpy golfers from trying to run a shot under the landscaping, a trap filled with thick rough guarded the front entrance. Charlie carded his second par in a row and captured the skin here. Jeff, who had not even picked up his golf clubs for a year and a half before that day, was already chastising himself for shooting bogey and double bogey on the first two holes.

Charlie continued to knock down pars on three and four, but Jeff and I each halved with him once, forcing the skins to carry over. Just to rile Charlie, I was tempted to remind him that he hadn't taken a bogey or a double bogey yet; instead, I asked what his secret was, an infinitely more subtle way of trying to make him self-conscious, of endeavoring to deflate any transcendence that might have crept into his game. Like a true northwesterner, he mumbled something about drinking two double *caffé lattes* before the round.

After only a few holes, it was clear that each of us really cared about winning this silly skins game, and that more was at stake than just a few dollars. The *idea* of winning assumed tremendous significance. Charlie, who is usually funny and extroverted, stared at the ground between shots, and I sensed that he was talking silently to his golf clubs. Jeff just shook his head ruefully. On the one hand, since I'd encouraged Jeff to come out with us that day, I was worried he might not be enjoying himself. On the other, I was equally concerned about Charlie beating me. I knew that if I lost even fifty cents, my day would lack the kind of expansiveness and the sense of justification I'd feel upon winning—as if some higher power had recognized and rewarded all my good works and pure intentions.

On the fifth hole, which featured an impossibly slanting domed green, Jeff scored his second par in a row, tying Charlie for the hole and adding another skin to the unclaimed pile. Jeff's breathing grew slow and deep as he strived to slip into a centered frame of mind, as he struggled to *be* the ball. But I knew that at Lakeview we were each likely to experience a few truly horrific holes, and the player who could shake these off was most likely to win. Knowing how hard Jeff is on himself—an instinct that has made him into a successful writer—and that Charlie could, on occasion, be expected to fling a golf club, I tried to relax and wait for my opportunity.

"Don't think of what you have to do, don't consider how to carry it out!" he exclaimed. "The shot will only go smoothly when it takes the archer himself by surprise."
—*Eugen Herrigel,* Zen in the Act of Archery

At ninety-nine yards, number six didn't appear to be a very tough hole. But if, for example, one of us were to loft an excellent wedge shot over the dense grove of trees directly in front of the green, and if that shot drifted just a shade to the left, that ball would settle at the bottom of a trap twelve feet deep. Getting out would be about as easy as standing on the street directly below a second-floor window and hitting a flop shot between the slats of the venetian blinds. I sincerely hoped that Jeff or Charlie might disappear into that pit; I anticipated the pleasure of watching their games unravel.

Even if you avoided the trap on your tee shot, the greenskeeper had placed the pin about four feet from a steep slope that ran right into the sand, so a putt might fall over the edge, too. Missing that green left you with a decision regarding whether to run your next shot at the pin, or simply to lay up halfway to the hole and hope to two-putt for bogey.

Charlie and I both carded pars on number six, forcing another carryover, but more important, extending his string of pars to six in a row. I was afraid I might be witnessing some kind of immaculate round, but I knew that eventually Charlie would think about that, too.

> "What are you thinking of," [the Master] would cry. "You know already that you should not grieve over bad shots; learn now not to rejoice over the good ones. You must free yourself from the buffetings of pleasure and pain, and learn to rise above them in easy equanimity, to rejoice as though not you but another had shot well. This, too, you must practice unceasingly—you cannot conceive how important it is."
> —*Eugen Herrigel,* Zen in the Art of Archery

I was relieved when Charlie bogeyed seven, but the best I could do was tie, pushing the skins on to eight, an eighty-two-yard blind hole over a couple of trees to a green that featured a rather unique hazard: a landscaped pond in its center. Charlie hit the back edge, leaving him to putt around the water toward a hole set on a downslope that slanted—where else?—directly toward the pond. I landed short and left my uphill putt close enough to tap in for par.

"This is really twisted," Jeff said—possibly because I won six skins on the hole. In spite of earning the contempt and enmity of my friends, I still felt wonderfully cocky.

On the ninth, seventy yards over a lake afloat with fake ducks, Jeff's tee shot missed the cup by no more than two inches, but then settled on the final micrometer of fringe before a steep trap. This was not proving to be his luckiest day. From where his ball lay, the green sloped steeply upward; if he didn't hit it hard enough, it might roll back past him into the trap. But once the slanting surface climbed to its apex, it sloped steeply down the other side, toward the water.

Jeff stood off to one side, examining his position. "It's not the putt I'm worried about," he said after a moment. "I'm afraid of falling into that trap and not being able to climb out."

Twenty feet from the pin, he was lucky to manage a four putt. Charlie also scored a five, and I stole the skin with a bogey.

The fact that the others truly and obviously cared about winning this match made each of us want to win even more, and I understood not only that winning was a mark of divine approval, but that we also figured, in our own ways, that winning would ensure the respect and approval of our opponents, and allow us to think better of ourselves as well. In this mire of competition and subjectivism, how we golfed at least partly determined who we were.

Charlie's steady play on the front nine earned him a

31—two strokes better than my score and eight better than Jeff's. I still managed to exude an attitude of moral superiority because I'd captured eight skins. Jeff looked at his watch as we walked off the ninth green, probably hoping we wouldn't want to play the back nine. That way he could escape the obvious fact that he hadn't golfed like Fred Couples in spite of not having touched his clubs in eighteen months.

Is it "I" who draw the bow, or is it the bow that draws me? . . . Do "I" hit the goal or does the goal hit me? . . . Bow, arrow, goal and ego, all melt into one another, so that I can no longer separate them. And even the need to separate has gone. For as soon as I take the bow and shoot, everything becomes so clear and straightforward and so ridiculously simple. . . .
—*Eugen Herrigel,* Zen in the Art of Archery

We forged ahead to the tenth, which was as close to a real golf hole as we saw all day: 173 yards around several trees to an elevated green. From there we returned to number two and played all the same holes, except that the back tees were placed in such a way that you couldn't see any of the greens. Which was a kind of advantage, considering the pin placements.

On eleven, our progress slowed when we caught a foursome of Hell's Angels, who played with burly, leather-clad precision.

"I'd bet anything that the greenskeeper gives free tattoos in the pro shop," Jeff commented as we watched them from the tee. By the way they measured their putts, I guessed that

71

these bikers had some sort of competition going, too—maybe for spark plugs. Or jail time.

I spent the rest of the back nine trying to catch Charlie, but he never lost his grip on the lead. He picked up five skins with a bogey on the sixteenth, and coasted to a 67 with eight pars and seven skins total. Jeff carded an unhappy 80, three pars, and no skins. I shot 72, with five pars and a birdie, but captured eleven skins.

In spite of the fact that Charlie beat me by five strokes, I walked off the last green confident that I was a better golfer—as if this really mattered in any way. I could afford a haughty attitude because I'd won the most money: about nine dollars. Of course, Charlie could probably muster the same attitude, because although he lost a couple of bucks to me, he still carded the lowest score. In fact, I'm almost certain that he also went home nurturing the idea that he'd won. Perhaps Jeff, too—reasoning that he hadn't played in so long, and therefore should have received a few handicap strokes—convinced himself that he was the winner. Which raises another interesting paradox: In a three-way match, how can all three participants claim victory?

Archery is not practiced solely for hitting the target; the swordsman does not wield the sword just for the sake of outdoing his opponent. . . .

If one really wishes to be master of an art, technical knowledge of it is not enough. One has to transcend technique so that the art becomes an "artless art" growing out of the Unconscious.

In the case of archery, the hitter and the hit are no longer two opposing objects, but are one reality. The archer ceases to be conscious of himself as the one who is engaged in hitting the bull's-eye which confronts him. This state of unconsciousness is realized only when, completely empty and rid of the self, he becomes one with the perfecting of his technical skill, though there is in it something of a quite different order which cannot be attained by any progressive study of the art.

—*From the Introduction to* Zen in the Art of Archery *by Daisetz T. Suzuki*

Bow and arrow are only a pretext for something that could just as well happen without them, only the way to a goal, not the goal itself, only help for the last decisive leap.

—*Eugen Herrigel,* Zen in the Art of Archery

To solve the paradoxes presented by the simultaneously competitive and transcendent aspects of golf, consider another paradox:

You cannot study Zen for the limited purpose of becoming a better golfer, because a successful student of Zen would not comprehend the notion of a "better" golfer, or even the idea of himself as a "successful" student. He would necessarily move beyond such subjective perceptions. In fact, in Zen, which strives for transcendence, any goal—such as scoring well, or even unraveling a koan—must necessarily fall away. The destination ceases to matter, and only the process of getting there, the journey itself, assumes importance. In answer to the question of who really won our golf match, the Head Pro might respond—in transcendent Zen fashion—simply, "Mu!" *Mu* is an untranslatable excla-

73

mation often used by Zen Master Joshu as a means of clearing his students' minds and detaching them from thoughts of the world.

On the other hand, you *can* study golf as a means of becoming more attuned to Zen, thereby perfecting your game; however, to consider the resulting improvement as any kind of end, as anything other than a meaningless aspect of the spiritual process—an aspect the consciousness of which you would have to transcend to achieve true mastery—would distort the art. It would be impure. Herrigel warns of "the danger of getting stuck in achievement, which is confirmed by success and magnified by renown: in other words, of behaving as if the artistic existence were a form of life that bore witness to its own validity."

Competition, by focusing on an end such as beating your opponent or shooting under par, is only a surface reflection of golf's true spirit. Zen golf lies beyond this obvious, manicured terrain—far beyond even the game itself, which is just a vehicle, and only one of many. Competition is what golf is usually about, but Zen is what it *can* be about. It is not the shot itself that matters, but rather the shooting. Zen focuses on *process,* on the journey that a round of golf constitutes.

This state, in which nothing definite is thought, planned, striven for, desired or expected, which aims in no particular direction and yet knows itself capable alike of the possible and the impossible, so unswerving is its power—this state, which is at bottom purposeless and egoless, was called by the Master truly "spiritual." It is in fact charged with spiritual awareness and is therefore also called "right presence of mind." This means that the mind or spirit is present everywhere, because it is nowhere attached to any particular place. And it can remain present because, even when related to this or that object, it does not cling to it by reflection and thus lose its original mobility. Like water filling a pond, which is always ready to flow off again, it can work its inexhaustible power because it is free, and be open to everything because it is empty.

—*Eugen Herrigel,* Zen in the Art of Archery

I realized these things long after our match at Lakeview Challenge, long after I spent my nine dollars in winnings on cold micro-brewed beers sipped on the deck of a restaurant overlooking the Willamette River, in Portland, Oregon. It required another long, strange trip to make these lessons clear, and over time, I'd need to learn the same things yet again:

The process
i s
The destination
i s
The journey
i s

THE END

CHAPTER FIVE

Golfing the Heart of Darkness

Gamesman: I believe I know what it is.
Layman: What do you mean?
Gamesman: I believe I know what you're doing.
Layman: What?
Gamesman: Yes. Why you're hitting them.
Straight left arm at the moment of impact.
Layman (pleased): I know what you mean. Oh,
God, yes! If the left arm isn't coming down
straight like a flail—
Gamesman: Rather.
Layman: Like a whip—
Gamesman: It's centrifugal force.
Layman: Well, I don't know. Yes, I suppose it is.
But if there's the least suggestion of—of—
Gamesman: A crooked elbow—(L. is framing up
to play his shot) Half a sec. Do you mind if I
come around to this side of you? I want to see

you play that shot. . . . (L. hits it) . . . Beauty.
(Pause).
Layman: Good Lord, yes! You've got to have a
straight left arm.
Gamesman: Yes. And even that one wasn't as
clean as some of the shots you've been
hitting. . . .
Layman (pleased): Wasn't it? (Doubtful) Wasn't
it? (He begins to think about it.)
   —*Stephen Potter,* The Theory and Practice of Gamesmanship

   One day assistant pro Chuang-tzu and a friend
were walking beside the river which flows along
the fairway of the sixth hole.
   "How delightfully the fishes are enjoying
themselves in the water!" Chuang-tzu exclaimed.
   "You are not a fish," his friend said. "How do
you know whether or not the fishes are enjoying
themselves?"
   "You are not me," Chuang-tzu said. "How do
you know that I do not know that the fishes are
enjoying themselves?"

—Zen golf koan

THE RAINY SEASON ANNOUNCED ITS IMMINENT ARRIVAL AS
we were finishing the fourteenth hole at the Ivoire Golf
Club, in Abidjan, Côte d'Ivoire, West Africa—an excellent,
rough-hewn golf course lined with towering silk trees and fragrant bougainvillea. The layout played 7,200 tough yards from
the back tees, but walking in that heat it might as well have
been 72,000. The course offered many formidable challenges,
not least of which was finishing while you were still alive.
   A mass of hot, soupy, humid air had hung above us all
afternoon, intensifying the fertile jungle atmosphere, weighing

77

down the tropical insects so they were too damp to fly. But on the fourteenth hole the sky began changing; our caddies looked nervously at the black reef of approaching clouds and muttered among themselves in a French as rich as dark-roasted coffee.

I turned to my new friend, Serge, from Toronto—one of eight golf journalists and tour operators who'd been invited on this press trip to promote, of all things, golf in Côte d'Ivoire—for a translation. He spoke English just a little bit like Inspector Clouseau.

"They say, 'Play fast,' " Serge said, glancing at his watch. " 'The rain comes in forty minutes.' " A sonic clap of thunder punctuated his pronouncement, and we both flinched.

Although probably in the minority, I secretly welcomed the rainy season, and the very *idea* of the rainy season, because it emphatically meant—without question, without mitigating circumstances, unequivocally—that there would be no more golf, at least for a while. I looked up at the charcoal sky with tremendous hope before sculling a short chip shot and then three-putting the fourteenth green.

Exactly thirty-four minutes later, just after we'd knocked our drives out onto the eighteenth fairway, a thin mist descended like a theater curtain falling, and shortly thereafter the punctual rain began—first in large, intermittent drops, and then in a pounding fusillade, a persistent staccato volley, like machine-gun fire. The drops impressed me with their weight and velocity, and felt soothingly cool in the oppressive heat.

Serge and I sprinted up the last fairway with irons in our hands, running across the sopping, spongy grass and around a vegetation-choked lake, attempting approach shots in the manner of polo players striking a ball on the move. The rain was dogged, but we finished the hole and reached the clubhouse as the downpour intensified. Two hundred yards behind us, the caddies shouldered our golf bags with calm determination, chins tucked toward their chests, orange jumpsuits turned rust-colored and heavy in the rain they'd known would come.

I welcomed the rainy season because, to my mind, it possessed the metaphorical power to cleanse and renew the world, and I most certainly needed cleansing and renewal: Over the past week I had somehow lost my golf game—and with it a part of my identity—in that hot, equatorial locale. Lost it, I slightly overdramatize, as Captain Kurtz lost himself in the African jungle in Joseph Conrad's *Heart of Darkness* (and in Francis Ford Coppola's film version, *Apocalypse Now*). Each time I addressed a golf ball that week, I heard Marlon Brando uttering Kurtz's mournful last words, as if commenting directly upon my game:

"The horror. The horror."

There are places on this planet—Scotland, for example—that almost magically plug us into a network of collective consciousness, that connect us to history or community, to the earth, or to ourselves. There are also places that inexplicably set us adrift, so lacking familiarity that they destroy our perspective until we lose ourselves in their strangeness. If we're adventurous, we may give in, let go, topple backward through the void and allow these places to transport us where they may. Letting go can help us see the world in fresh new ways and open ourselves to change. But letting go is also dangerous; we don't know what lurks within the unmanicured terrain beyond our preconceptions, and once we venture into that darkness, we can't be certain we'll ever be able to reclaim our previous views of the world and of ourselves—views that may constitute an important component of who we are. Captain Kurtz allowed himself to become so dramatically and permanently untethered in the African jungle that he could never live in the Western European world of civilized men again.

For me, Côte d'Ivoire was just such a disorienting place, though whether due to some dark African power, or as a result of the country's own identity crisis, or simply because I *wished* it to have this kind of effect, I can't be sure. Whatever the reason, my golf game was lost to me there, and while this sounds trivial, its implications penetrated deep: losing my game became the first step in a process of losing myself— which I failed to recognize at the time was exactly what I needed. I wouldn't have chosen golf as the impetus for a personal crisis and ultimate revelation; I'd have preferred something more sensational—an international political intrigue, or a pitched battle and chase with hungry though respectful cannibals—but sometimes we must make use of the opportunities we're given.

Thinking about Africa before my trip began, I had pined for darkness and everything it could teach me. I had hungered for the kind of night journey that Kurtz underwent, and that Marlow experienced in seeking out Kurtz. I wished to abandon myself to primitive tribal customs and denounce the hollow rituals of my own culture. I had wanted to face the dangers of going native, and delve into my own dark subcontinent. I ached to become a Wild Man.

But, unfortunately, I hadn't traveled to Côte d'Ivoire on a journey of discovery. I hadn't come to Africa to experience the richness of a primal society so alien to my own, to feel the pounding drumbeats of the jungle, the black magic, the tribal viscerousness of a continent the very name of which conjures up fear of disease and hardship and incivility and the unknown.

I'd come to the heart of darkness to play golf. I'd been brought to this small country wedged between the savanna and the sea by Côte d'Ivoire's Ministry of Tourism, and by Air Afrique, to promote two resort hotels and golf courses—an aim so naive and silly and hopeful and self-deceptive that I was awed by it, in the same way I was awed by the earnest hospitality of my African hosts. Yet the very notion that they hoped to sell this hot, desolate country as a golf destination for Americans implied that Côte d'Ivoire faced a rather dramatic identity crisis of its own.

I understood this better after reading various brochures and public relations materials that referred to the country as "the African Riviera" and called the largest city, Abidjan, "the Tropical Manhattan" and "the Paris of West Africa," as if they really couldn't decide what they wanted Côte d'Ivoire to be. It became more apparent when I visited the posh Hotel Ivoire in Abidjan, which boasts a bowling alley, indoor ice-skating rink, and other amenities that suggested this third-world nation was also trying to sell itself as a kind of misplaced Catskills resort: "Borscht Belt in the Bush," perhaps.

But Côte d'Ivoire's identity crisis was most clearly expressed by the city of Yamoussoukro, home to the Hotel President Golf Club, the Hotel President, and the Basilica of Nôtre Dame de la Paix.

The Hotel President Golf Club—a well-groomed, American-style layout set in a pastoral savanna surrounded by pineapple plantations, full of blossoming magnolias and flamboyant trees, and aflutter with bright yellow birds—is simply a well-designed, challenging golf course like you might come across in Palm Springs.

The Hotel President is merely a fine, well-kept property, similar to hotels you'd find throughout Europe.

The Basilica of Nôtre Dame de la Paix is something altogether otherworldly.

Built in three years, at a cost of $300 million (most of the nation's treasury), by President Felix Houphouët-Boigny, the basilica was designed to rival St. Peter's in Rome and attract Catholics from around the globe. Although the original plans called for the dome to reach higher than St. Peter's, the Ivorians amended this intention at the Pope's request. But when they finally placed a gold cross on top, Nôtre Dame de la Paix was slightly taller.

By any measure, the basilica is an incomparable monument, so overwhelmingly beautiful you must sit down inside just to catch your breath. Aside from the elegant marble pillars and carved stonework, the floor mosaics and the bone-white, gold-topped cupola that seems from a distance to hover hugely above the Earth, it is the stained-glass windows a visitor will never forget. Thirty-six of them cover 8,000 square meters, reaching from floor to ceiling in 4,000 different shades and hues of color that, as the sun shifts or clouds drift by, flow through the circular structure like a kaleidoscopic river of pure, ethereal light, shimmering, mesmerizing, hypnotic, reaching up to a round stained-glass roof that seems illumined by heaven itself.

With such a fantastical attraction as the basilica, as well as excellent accommodations and great golf, the only thing Ya-moussoukro lacks is visitors. During an hour at the basilica, we didn't encounter another soul. In the middle of a perfectly fine golf day, our group constituted the only two foursomes on the golf course. And back at the hotel—which has a 5 percent occupancy rate—our footsteps rang eerily in the deserted lobby. For the two days we visited, the elegant eight-lane boulevards—boulevards to rival the Champs Elysées, boulevards lined with 10,000 lights—were also empty. Just outside of the district, many of them dead-ended in the jungle.

The Ivorians built it all, but nobody has come, leaving them to wonder why the rest of the world has not chosen to see Yamoussoukro—indeed, the whole of Côte d'Ivoire—as the locals might have hoped, and providing a sort of textbook example of what Eastern philosophers might call maya, or illusion, a false sense of reality. Perhaps it's even led the Ivorians to question who they really are. The golf course, the hotel, the basilica, the entire empty city seem to have nothing to do with Africa the dark continent. Is that notion just a myth? Have they left it behind to history? Or is the modern Ivorian self-image somehow miscast? In fact, aren't all self-images somehow miscast?

In spite of these strange circumstances, which seemed to betray the very nature and identity of Africa (or at least how I thought of Africa); in spite of spending most of my time in Côte d'Ivoire on golf courses and in luxurious hotels, the African darkness I sought reached me anyway, weirdly enough, through golf. I wanted a powerful tribal journey, but ended up spending most of my time out on the links. So the golf courses became a path to that true dark continent, which always lies within us.

Drivers wracked by images of limitation and self-doubt develop a mind set that not only interferes with awareness and the dexterity needed to avoid a collision, but actually creates a kind of self-fulfilling prophecy: If you expect to hit something eventually, you eventually just might.

—*K. T. Berger,* Zen Driving

Before arriving in Côte d'Ivoire, I'd owned a dependable level of golf mediocrity—a consistent if unpretty swing I could usually count on, and a confidence that enabled me to play, if not awesomely, at least respectably. I knew the feel of a well-struck shot that flies off the club face as you follow through. But on the first tee of the Ivoire Golf Club, with our entire group gathered together for a photo, something in me had already changed. Something I'd been able to stand sturdily upon in this world had given way, though it took me a few days to realize the extent—and the implications—of my loss.

I should have seen the early signs. For example: With everyone watching, I knocked my very first African tee shot into the jungle. Walking out toward where it disappeared, I ignored my caddy's mimed advice to simply forget it and drop another ball. I thought he was just being lazy, so I approached and parted the vegetation with my three wood—if not to find my ball, then at least to show my caddy I couldn't be pushed around.

A moment later, I heard a loud rustling in the brush, a VERY LOUD AND CLUMSY RUSTLING IN THE BRUSH, as if some huge creature were rooting around, looking for dumb golfers to snack on. My caddy peered in cautiously and then backed away. Quickly. He began yelling at me in French. He pointed to the extra ball he'd given me, demanding I use it.

84

"Geez, what did you see?" I asked him, sure that he'd at least glimpsed the animal that had made that noise. Rhino? I wondered. Elephant? *Lion?*

He raised one hand and moved it in a slithering, serpentine motion, muttering a single word in French, which I somehow understood.

"A *snake?*" I said.

"Snake. Yes," he said, and held his hands parallel, three feet apart, the way you show someone how big the fish was that got away. From the noise the snake had made, I knew my caddy was indicating its *width*.

Snakes in the garden have been a bad omen for many years now, so I should have realized that something unpleasant was marching down the pike. Or maybe the bees should have served to warn me that I was on the reservation list for some bad golf karma, which may have been due me from the way I'd clung to practical, subsidiary aims, rather than embracing more spiritual goals, during my recent competition at Duke's Lakeview Challenge. The fact was that even by the time I'd gotten to Africa, I hadn't fully learned my Zen lessons; it took reflecting after the fact upon my African golf/personality crisis to teach me, fully and intrinsically, what the Lakeview Challenge had offered. My experience in Africa was an example of what could happen if you failed to look beyond limited goals, if you failed to focus on the journey rather than on some destination. But in this case, there was something more as well.

The bees were peacefully and invisibly nesting on the underside of a palm leaf in the rough along the seventh fairway, completely minding their own business, not even looking for trouble. But my errant drive came to rest directly under that particular palm leaf, so I had to hold it aside with my body

to hit my next shot—though I would certainly have been glad
to take a penalty stroke had I known the bees were there. The
bees were not happy about the disturbance, and neither was
my caddy, who began shouting at me again and waving his
arms. He later explained to Serge, in French, that a single
sting from one of these bees could swell you up like a sausage.
But he wasn't half as unhappy as he'd be when he started
betting on me, against Serge, with Serge's caddy.

I soon discerned that these particular natural hazards at the
Ivoire Golf Club were mere metaphors for the real trouble—
internal, psychological trouble, an identity crisis not unlike
Côte d'Ivoire's—that was still to come. During that first
round of golf, and during an equally horrendous performance
the following day, I discovered myself in possession of a golf
game I neither recognized nor acknowledged as my own, a
game that not only embarrassed me in front of my colleagues,
but which eventually led me to question whether I was really
the golfer I'd imagined myself to be.

At first, of course, it just seemed like bad golf. But in the
same way that an obsessive-compulsive can't help focusing on
something he doesn't want to focus on—constantly washing
his hands like Lady Macbeth, for instance—or in much the
same way that you can't resist probing a loose and aching tooth
with your tongue, I began to think about my bad golf, to
accept it, almost to embrace it, until hitting a good shot
seemed like the most hopelessly unlikely occurrence in the
world. In the middle of my backswing, I'd hear a voice telling
me I was going to top the ball, top the ball, top the ball, that
I wasn't good enough to hit a decent shot. And then, not
surprisingly, I'd top the ball, and slip down another stratum
into this weird abyss.

Over those first few days I tried revising various aspects of my grip, stance, backswing, downswing, shoulder angle, wrist turn, and other components of the golf swing that I'd learned about at the Innisbrook Golf Institute, searching for some key, something I could rely on again, looking for a solid core around which I could rebuild my game, regain my confidence and my vision of who I was as a golfer.

I have never been the type of person who performs badly and then lets this performance grow larger than it merits. I more than occasionally play a bad round of golf and manage to forget about it. But in Côte d'Ivoire, one bad round of golf segued into another and then another, successively washing away my confidence the way an extremely high storm tide eats away the sand bank supporting a beach house until the structure finally collapses and washes out to sea. In Côte d'Ivoire, it was as if I stood on the beach watching the inevitable erosion of my game, but was powerless to stop it.

In the realm of the obvious, the core of my problem was this: At some level, I still believed that my golf game at least partly reflected the kind of person I was—if not to myself (I should know better), then at least to others. If I'd lived cleanly and well, and with discipline; if I'd managed to overcome self-consciousness and strived for transcendence in my activities and thoughts; if everything was right with my world, then I should have been able to shoot a good round of golf. I should have been able to exert the same kind of influence over my game that I employed in my life, thus proving myself to be a certain kind of person, because golf and life happen to require some of the same skills.

In cases where this somewhat ridiculous philosophy doesn't stand up, I can usually manage to rationalize why my game doesn't reflect my life. When I'm the only one watching, or if I'm golfing with a companion who knows me, it's all right not to play well; we both know who I am, and a bad round of golf can't undermine that. Or if I know I'll never see the folks I'm playing with again, my performance doesn't matter so much.

But at some level, seeing ourselves in a particular way involves believing that other people see us in a similar light. We create our self-images partly based on how teammates and opponents, coworkers and family members, friends, and strangers on buses see us—or at least how we perceive they do. And if something informs us that our self-image doesn't jibe with how others see us, we can revamp that part of our self-image if honesty and realism are important to us. Ultimately, of course, we need to let go of such views entirely— that's the true solution to this dilemma, and further evidence supporting the lessons I had learned (but not yet completely) at Duke's. But sometimes the true path is overgrown and not at all clear to us. Sometimes we become entangled at the level of metaphor and forget to step beyond it. My experience in Africa was like summer school, meant to teach me the essential lessons I'd failed to learn earlier, by providing an example of where the route of subjectivism could lead.

> Succeed without taking credit,
> And have no desire to display their excellence.
> —*Tao Te Ching*, no. 72

By my third day of golf in Côte d'Ivoire, I couldn't bribe a golf ball to take its normal, lovely flight. I mis-hit nearly every painful shot, and actually carded above a 120, as if I'd never played the game before. The other golf writers in my foursome—folks who didn't know me—must have held a very different image of me than the one I had of myself, at least as a golfer. The additional harm of this lay in the fact that I was equating myself as a golfer with myself as a person, so you can see where this began to lead. I was afraid that by seeing me as a guy who couldn't hit a decent golf shot, they would judge me harshly as a person—inept, inadequate, a fake. It was as if my twisted perception of what might have been their unenlightened perception could determine my identity, because in moments of weakness or sheer, unmitigated stupidity, *I* might think this way. Based on my perception of their possible perceptions of me, and based on that philosophical tenet "I shank, therefore I am," I truly began to doubt myself, but even worse, I thought the solution was to recapture my sense of who I imagined myself to be.

Somewhere in my past, deeply buried, lies an event or a memory that must have caused me to worry far too much about what other people might be thinking of me. Years of therapy have not exhumed the source of this, although by expending tremendous psychic energy I've mostly been able to cast this troubling, destructive tendency aside. But whatever hurt originally created this self-consciousness—whether it was my schoolmates laughing at me because I loved to wear psychedelic leather-fringed vests and medallions in the sixth grade; or that early on, before the world changed me, I was a hypersensitive child who *felt* everything; or maybe because certain people in my life were so critical of me that I internalized this criticism and became the critic myself— the root of this behavior pattern is still hidden away, exiled to some dark, interior continent of my psyche. But every now and then, something from the outside world drifts along and lands on the shore of that continent, like a ship lost at sea, and in so doing brings this dark tendency back to light. My loss of control on the golf courses of Côte d'Ivoire was just such a floundering ship.

But just as connecting with my father requires interpreting his golf talk not as a failure to communicate with me, but as a means of expressing affection, and just as correcting my swing at Innisbrook required perceiving my swing path differently, therapy might have suggested that I "change the tape" that I was hearing in Africa regarding my golf game reflecting my life. Or, in other words, that I change my perception. Zen, however, would take this notion even further by recommending that I throw away the tape player entirely, and that was the lesson I was struggling to learn: to let go of the concern that other people were seeing me in a certain way, but also to give up the ego attachment of how I saw myself, and just to *be*.

In Côte d'Ivoire, afraid of being judged as someone so different from who I know myself to be, I began to make excuses for my horrendous play. One morning, golfing with three of the others, I explained on the first tee that I'd never played so badly in my life, and didn't know what was happening. Maybe it was jet lag, I posited. Or the heat. Later in that same round I became self-deprecating. Upon knocking two balls into the water fronting a rather short, scenic par three—the kind of hole you want so much to play well—I said, "Now there's a surprise!" After hooking a long iron into the shrubbery two holes later, I mused, "I wonder what it would feel like to hit one straight." Throughout that round I grew by turns silent, angry, irritable, and earnest; while my moods swung wildly, however, I'm sure I consistently managed to annoy my playing partners. All because I so wanted these friendly strangers to see me differently than I imagined they were seeing me—as if they actually might have been as shallow as I was being, and judging me according to my golf. As if such limited views had anything to do with reality, were more than just maya, and actually mattered.

At some point toward the end of the week, when I'd virtually exhausted frustration, I grew even more terribly self-conscious, realizing that I'd been acting so out of character. Not long after my golf game took flight, my personality seemed to have followed it out the window. I felt helplessly lost, without confidence, unworthy, as if people were whispering behind my back and children were laughing at me again. I felt even more desperate to recover my game, as if by doing so I could reclaim my identity, when in fact I needed to let go of this identity.

> I am told that a pearl is produced only through the pearl-oyster's enduring the pain of having a grain of sand bore into its flesh, fighting against it, and protecting itself against it. We, also, by fighting all kinds of difficulties and overcoming them, strive to develop the jewel of spiritual cultivation.
>
> —*Isshu Miura and Ruth Fuller Sasaki,* The Zen Koan

A month or so after my strange trip to Côte d'Ivoire, I'd repaired that listing ship and set it back on a positive course. I regained my confidence and my golf game by transcending any outward, biased, or subjective views (or any views at all, for that matter) of my game. I went to the driving range and hit balls without worrying about where they went—without worrying about how I might have looked to anyone watching me, or even to myself. I focused instead on the process of swinging, ignoring all thoughts of good or bad. On the golf course, I simply played golf, and enjoyed the activity, the journey of walking in the grass for five hours.

In looking back at my identity crisis in Africa, I realized that you can take metaphors—golf as life, for instance—a little too far. And in other ways you can fail to take them far enough, to move beyond the level of metaphor and transcend such notions entirely. I learned, not for the first time, that you must put aside what you think other people might be thinking of you, because you can't know for sure anyway; but you must also put aside what other people *are* thinking, because it doesn't matter. And you must even put aside the destructively self-conscious ways you think about yourself. I also recognized, to my own surprise, that my particular crisis of identity was probably the exact kind of experience that leads some people to cheat at golf.

Most people like to see themselves, if not necessarily as winners, then at least as decent, solid participants in whatever they do. Because many of us perceive golf as a sport that somehow manages to express an aspect of who we are, some golfers need to see themselves as competent players, regardless of any evidence to the contrary—a view that may cause them to fudge their scores in an effort to protect that self-image, even if it is false to the core. Such players cannot give up their limiting ego attachments.

If a player likes to see himself as the kind of golfer who never shoots over 100, he can make his score come out to a 98 on a bad day even if the actual number might have been ten strokes higher. Paradoxically, in preserving his false self-image, he promulgates the opposite image to anyone who plays with him, and creates a very different reality. Other golfers don't see him as the guy who never shoots over 100, but as the guy who never *admits* to shooting over 100, even when he does.

A gulf develops between how he sees himself and who he really is. He alters his reality to fit his false self-image. After missing a three-foot putt he tells himself—and no doubt believes—that it was really a gimme, and he didn't actually concentrate for that reason, and so he scores the hole as if he'd made the putt. Or maybe to prove his integrity, he does it over, concentrating this time, but after pulling it left a second time he tells himself that it really *was* a gimme, why make such a big deal, take the par and be happy. Or he loses a ball in the rough just off the fairway and rationalizes taking a free drop because that ball really shouldn't have been lost. Maybe it plugged, or perhaps the grass should have been shorter to be really fair, or maybe the other players in his group didn't make much of an effort to help him find it. So he drops without penalty, rationalizing to protect his self-image.

He's probably not consciously trying to cheat. In fact, he may not even be aware of it as such. But it can be so painful and even psychically dangerous to admit that reality isn't backing up his self-image that, rather than substituting a more honest image (or making lame excuses, as I did in Africa), he alters reality to back the self-image he clings to. It may just be too scary to face something that threatens his very notion of who he is. It may be too frightening to let go of ego attachment, which has buoyed his self-image for a lifetime, not knowing what might happen to him if he allows it to sink to the bottom of consciousness and disappear, if he allows himself to exist independently of golf or any other false measure.

The place we could truly lose ourselves is at the very same point where we could demonstrate strength and resolve, and reaffirm who we are beyond golf or anything else. We could accomplish this by not *needing* to reaffirm or even consciously acknowledge an illusion such as who we are. By contrast, we lose ourselves by allowing ourselves to be lost, by putting so much stock in our golf game or in the type of car we drive or in where we went to college. We lose ourselves by giving other people the power—in our own minds—to judge us according to such things. Or by judging ourselves according to such shallow, meaningless measures, and succumbing to maya.

Those of us who aren't yet fully enlightened construct self-images that we're scared to mess with, even when reality points out their flaws. These self-images are the personal equivalents of Côte d'Ivoire's golf courses and hotels and basilica, built on our own internal dark continent, our own private Africa. But no matter what the extent of our constructions, our true natures succeed in expressing themselves, and we must be open to this, to changing and transcending our perceptions, to the fluid nature of true reality. Much of what truly defines us and expresses that nature is how we face the encroaching darkness, the thick jungle closing in to envelop what we've built. We can cheat or make excuses; face the darkness with bravado or with cynicism; or simply display quiet humility and move forward without a word, secure in who we are because that personality is undefined. The golfer who accomplishes this plays the game best beyond the fairway, where golf *can* say something about the people we are.

> Don't push. The situation will develop at its own
> pace. . . .
> The cycles in life cannot be hastened.
>
> —I Ching, *no. 24*

CHAPTER SIX

Because the Night

You must see for yourself
The reed-flowers drenched in moonlight
—*From Toyo Eicho Zenji's sixteenth-century compilation,*
A Phrase Book

Assistant pro Deshan was sitting cross-legged
on the ground outside the pro shop.
"Why don't you go home?" asked the Head
Pro.
"Because it is dark," answered Deshan.
The Head Pro fetched a candle and lit it, and
then handed it to Deshan, but as Deshan was
about to take it, the Head Pro blew it out.
Deshan had a sudden realization, and bowed.
—*Zen golf koan*

Because the Night

WHEN I WAS A SENIOR IN COLLEGE, MY FRIENDS AND I
achieved absolute mastery over one small aspect of golf:
Regardless of the season, we knew at precisely what time we
needed to tee off on the Vassar Golf Course to be the last
group out on any given day, and still hit into the final green
with enough daylight to watch our approach shots flying toward the pin. As the last foursome, we captured a mild sense
of moral superiority that remained hidden in shadows during
the heat of the crowded day, emerging only close to darkness.
We also enjoyed an unhurried freedom, a sense that the golf
course belonged solely to us. It served as our meditation retreat, a private classroom where we pursued and studied golf's
less obvious lessons. After tapping in on that final hole, if we
departed at a dead run with our clubs, we could usually reach
the campus dining center with just enough time to inhale two
dinners each and drink a cup of coffee before closing time.

Ever since college, I've preferred to finish my golf in the
whispery, muted light of dusk; to stand in the soft green grass
as the day fades into evening and the air cools and the night
birds commence calling and the eighteenth flag stirs—barely
visible, like a sailboat on the horizon—in the dim continuum
of time and distance and space. Golfing at that mystical hour
of transition, coming in after all other players have finished
and gone home, cutting as close to darkness as possible, is a
way of stepping into the fringe beyond the fairway where light
and shadows meld, where emerald grass and blue sky and
lavender sunset blend together toward the indistinguishable
color of the night, where everything merges into an encompassing Oneness; but the process of merging, and not yet the
Oneness itself, defines the moment.

Over the years, misjudging the timing of that fading coppery light on golf courses from Florida to Phuket has offered its own unexpected rewards. For example: Playing alone on the Boulders Resort's South course just before dusk on a warm, lovely Arizona evening, I saw two coyotes come loping out of the desert as I walked toward my errant tee shot on the par-three sixth hole. They stood for what seemed a long time in the lush grass, staring at me and—I swear—smiling. I gazed back until they eventually trotted off into the gathering dark. Then I turned to my ball and pitched it over a tree and a yawning bunker; it bounced twice and plunked into the hole. Somewhere in the desert, the coyotes yipped.

On other evenings, in other locales, scrambling down from the eighteenth tee just a little later than anticipated, I've occasionally played my final approach shot into fresh darkness purely on faith, without being able to see where my golf ball might land, figuring that if I struck it well the shot would travel where I aimed it—an exercise in transcendence that I highly recommend. And if all was right with the darkening world on such an evening, as lights twinkled in the clubhouse dining room and stars blinked on in the sky above, I'd find my ball no farther than a pitch away as I walked up toward the hole. Putting at that hour also revealed its own elusive secret: that a white ball absorbs any available light, and rolls across the dark backdrop of the green like a planet orbiting across a dark sky.

Some people prefer to golf early, in the bare, untested bright light of morning; that is something I'll never understand. When my father was still a bachelor, he and his friends used to go out for a few drinks on a Saturday night and then drive to the golf course at Eisenhower Park, on Long Island, at two A.M. They'd sleep in their cars (or stay up all night

smoking cigarettes) so they could be the first group to tee off
on Sunday morning, just after dawn. They'd finish by ten, with
the rest of the day stretching open before them.

But I prefer the hours leading imperceptibly toward darkness, which offer both meditative privacy and a sense of clo-
sure. At twilight, you can't play another nine holes even if
you want to. Nature and the golf course and the rotation of
the Earth conspire to say, "You must rest now. Stow your
clubs in the cluttered trunk of your car among the jumper
cables and wiffle balls and bags of salt for winter driving, at
least until morning. Think about your game. Reflect."

After the sun has dropped beyond the edge of the visible world
and the last putt has fallen into the cup, the golf course belongs to
darkness, to the animals that step carefully out of the woods,
browsing the shrubbery and sometimes howling at the round,
white, dimpled moon; to the cool vagaries of weather and temperature; to the slow breathing of the grass pushing up through
divots and ball marks. Cart paths grow slick with dew and birds
settle on the water hazards to feed, and the course transforms into
a place of pure potential—a place where anything can happen,
but not until tomorrow. For now, all action ceases, stillness en-
velops the topography, green fades to gray. Under cover of darkness, the golf course renews itself, free of golfers trampling
through in spiked shoes annoying the fragile sod.

Like so many places beyond the fairway, I've often envisioned the golf course at night as a tremendously romantic
location. I've dreamed of lying on the soft grass on a warm
evening with a bottle of good, cold wine and a woman I love,
watching the stars flicker and reel. I've imagined stealing away
from a party at some country club with my dream lover while
the other guests are dancing to "Twist and Shout," and head-

ing cross-country to a far-off green surrounded by gentle Scottish mounds, where the music sounds like distant wind chimes, and stately oaks and pines blot out the light. My lover and I would roll passionately across the putting surface, breaking left or right with the slope, locked in an embrace. We'd knock the flag stick over in our passion, and run barefoot through the bunkers without raking them. When we returned to the party an hour later, in time for dessert, our clothes would be rumpled—my white shirt and her tight-fitting dress tinged the bright color of new grass.

Dreamed of this, yes, but never pursued it. Even at Vassar, where it might have seemed so natural to stroll in moonlight beyond the fairway with a willing date, I never asked a woman out to the golf course at night (and none asked me). Whether because of some perceived sacredness, or because my girlfriends weren't golfers and might not have considered the seventh green a romantic location, or perhaps because my thesis advisor lived in a house along the course, I don't know. Maybe I felt that making love out there could only complicate both golf *and* romance, which were complex enough already. Maybe I figured that such unmanicured terrain was best left to the night, that playing into late twilight was my way of testing the barrier of darkness without plunging into it like a diver swanning into water the depth of which he doesn't know.

To know that you do not know is best
To not know of knowing is a disease.
—*Tao Te Ching,* no. 71

But times change, and if we're open-minded, we can change and expand our perceptions, too. As I've grown older I've

100

learned to test such limits, to push beyond them. Which explains how one August evening I found myself driving in my friend Charlie Blanchette's Volkswagen Jetta toward the Sahahlee Golf Course in Clackamas, Oregon, to play in a glow-ball tournament in the dark heart of the night (as opposed to playing in Africa, in the heart of darkness). Charlie was not exactly my dream lover, and knocking an iridescent ball around a par-three layout wasn't among the highest-quality golf experiences possible. But if playing golf in twilight represents a step toward fringes, then golfing in the dark, however silly, impractical, and potentially hazardous, involves moving beyond an obvious and powerful barrier—and one which I'd always avoided—deep into unmanicured terrain. Golfing in the dark was another golf koan, and I wanted to explore what it might reveal.

The sun was plunging toward Oregon's coastal mountains and the sky ranged from delicate tangerine to velvety blue when Charlie and I arrived at Sahahlee. Dozens of golfers sat around the clubhouse porch on a bluff high above the golf course, eating barbecued hamburgers, drinking beer from cans, and watching shadows lengthen and converge. Waiting for last light to leach out of the clear western sky.

Half an hour later, when the darkness thickened and a wedge of crescent moon hovered just above a distant ridge of pines, a horn signaled that we should report to our respective starting holes. Charlie and I merged with the crowd shuffling like cattle down steep switchbacks. Far below us, the green glow-lights marking tees and flag sticks stood out like the vapor lights burning along an airport runway at night. We taxied toward number seventeen, nearly crashing into two couples who, we soon discovered, composed the rest of our group.

The seventeenth hole, from where we'd been assigned to tee off, was actually labeled as number twelve, which might have proven confusing had not one member of our group played much of his golf here, at Sahahlee, at night. He explained that the tournament director generally excluded five of Sahahlee's eighteen holes from competition because they featured water hazards—although whether this decision was intended to prevent the loss of expensive glow-balls or to protect night-blind golfers from drowning, I never figured out. The remaining holes were subsequently renumbered from one to thirteen.

As we waited on the tee for the signal to begin playing, the six of us prepared our glow-balls by removing small plastic tubes from the foil packets we'd been given, and bending them until something inside broke, causing two chemicals to mix and emit a sort of radioactive glow. Then we inserted the thin tubes into hollow channels in our special plastic golf balls.

Standing in the dark among strangers, with that weird, luminous sphere in my hand, I reflected on the fact that so many people had come out here to play golf at an hour when most sensible folks were probably lying back on their sofas or sitting in a comfortable bar. It struck me as just a little cultish until I realized that many golfers would play the game in virtually any conceivable conditions—underwater, perhaps, or atop an active volcano—because golfing *is* a cult, an addiction, and golfers compose a fanatical order of loonies running around with sticks in their hands. This may be so because the game teaches us about ourselves and the world around us, and in different circumstances—such as in the jungle, or on the toughest par-three course in the world;

playing with our dads, or against lifelong rivals, or on world-class championship layouts—the lessons vary as widely as the terrain. Golfing in the dark was just one more variable that might offer insight on the game, and beyond it. Also, in Oregon, many people apparently have nothing better to do on a Saturday night.

When the starter's horn finally emitted its plaintive *ah-ooh-ga* again from the clubhouse a short time later, the moon had slipped beneath the ridge line and the dark sky popped incandescently with tiny stars. Charlie teed off first in our group, and hit a shot that accelerated through the dark atmosphere like a meteor. Within moments, comets and shooting stars flew in green trajectories all around us, arcing, turning groundward, bouncing, finally settling in glowing green pools in the grass.

We stood awestruck, like astronomy students watching the Perseid meteor shower streaking across the sky.

"What did you hit?" I asked Charlie when his ball eventually crashed back to earth.

"I have no idea. I can't see the numbers on my clubs." He paused before adding, "But that doesn't really matter, because I can't tell how far the hole is, anyway."

I consulted the scorecard in the light emitted by my glowing ball. "A hundred and sixty-four yards," I said.

"Then it must have been a six iron."

I took out my own six iron, reminding myself to swing easy. I addressed my fluorescent ball without performing my customary pre-shot routine, because that involved actually being able to see both where I was and where I was aiming. I reminded myself that it was the journey that mattered, the process of playing, not where my ball ended up.

If keeping your head down is a critical element of a normal golf shot struck during the day, its importance increases exponentially in the dark. Once you've set your stance, the entire swing must happen automatically, without benefit of corrections along the way. If your golf game relies on excellent hand-eye coordination, or the split-second timing (based on visual cues) common to imperfect swings, at night you'll find yourself suddenly transformed into a Neanderthal of form and execution—because in the blinding darkness you swing a ghost golf club that you cannot see. Only the ball is visible. And if you happen to look up from your ball into the distance, and then back at it, your pupils will still be reacting to the change in lighting, assuring the total distortion of any vision you might have had, as when you gaze into a camera flash in a dimly lit room. So the darkness provides a perfect exercise in transcendence, and also in visualization—a technique I learned about some months later, on a golf trip through the Rocky Mountains in winter (see Chapter Seven).

I didn't really comprehend these lessons until about the third hole at Sahahlee (which was actually the second hole of the golf course, although that night it was labeled as number one because the real number-one hole contained water and wasn't in play), after topping my first fifteen or sixteen shots. I'd been far more interested in watching the gorgeous green trajectory of my ball than in hitting a good shot, more concerned with the ball's flight than where it landed; that became apparent from the way I kept staring off into the distance before my club even made contact, virtually assuring a series of forty-yard rollers.

It took our group a long while to play the first few holes—which didn't really matter, because it wasn't as if we had to finish before dark. Tracer bullets of green light streaked through the night around us, and mysterious whoops and yips and coyote barks echoed across the valley. The darkness was so enveloping that you couldn't even see a golfer actually hitting a ball: You'd be staring at a glowing green sphere in the grass and it would appear simply to launch itself into flight, as if golfer, club, and glowing ball had truly become one. When all the members of our group had knocked their glow-balls within putting distance on any particular hole, the lights stood clustered together like bright golf constellations: the Shark, the Walrus, the Golden Bear, Little Ben.

If ever I've slipped so deep into self-absorption to imagine that I've learned even a fraction of what golf has to teach me, playing in the dark revealed a thousand subtle new lessons: simple ones, like remembering to keep track of where I set my golf clubs so I could find them again; lessons of physics, such as that no matter how deep into the woods you slice a glow-ball, it will still beckon to you with a faint orb of green light (I found this to be true in shallow water as well); and essential lessons appropriate to both day and night golf, such as keeping your eye on the ball and believing in your own swing. This kind of unconditional faith, and an accompanying attitude of self-confidence, are the cornerstones of a respectable golf game, and striving for them is an excellent way to go through life. As soon as I understood this, I began unleashing bright, blazing comets into the darkness at Sahahlee, although some of mine had a tendency to enter irregular orbits, causing them to veer sharply in a clockwise direction.

This night golf koan also revealed what an utterly solitary game golf is, particularly in the dark. Charlie and I played with the others for nearly three hours, and when we exchanged sleepy good-byes just after midnight, we still had no idea what they looked like. Darkness accentuated the golfer's tendency to inhabit interior, private space. Why talk to someone you can't even see? It also made the game a more intimate, personal, even individualistic form of moving meditation. We were each very much alone with our shots.

Although I was not particularly disappointed when the tournament ended, there was something weirdly and undeniably spiritual about golfing in the dark. Somehow, the flight of our glow-balls provided a metaphor for our own travel through this vast, unknown universe. That luminous ball was our beacon through the black void, a ship launched into the unknown, a candle set adrift on a river of darkness. Which is another way of saying that playing golf at night involves confronting something far larger and more complex than ourselves, an encompassing power that we must submit to rather than struggle against, a force that may allow us to merge with golf and the dark and other disparate elements, into Oneness.

After thirteen holes of glow-ball, I also understood that, occasionally, the edges of things—such as golfing at twilight— may prove more engaging, more romantic, more intrinsically full of metaphorical value and real pleasure than what lies beyond them, in the same way that coastlines are beautiful even to folks who don't care for the ocean. Sometimes a venture into unmanicured terrain leaves us craving fringes, or even fairways. What's most important, however, is the process of exploration, that instinct to move beyond, regardless of what we discover when we arrive there. And it's equally essential to preserve that instinct even when we don't embrace where it leads us. Though I learned a few things from golfing in the dark, I still prefer playing at dusk.

Glow-ball, I quickly discovered, was no substitute for my romantic visions regarding what can happen on a golf course in the dark, just as golf is no substitute for lovemaking—at least not if the golf takes place at night. I'd still rather play in twilight; if I must be on the links in darkness, I'd prefer the company of someone who doesn't care—at that particular, romantic hour—about golf.

CHAPTER SEVEN

A Winter's (Golf) Tale

Visualization is an active form of meditation in which you relax and choose to view images in your mind's eye that will influence your emotions and energy. Visualization is a natural process. It lets you tap into your inner sources of peace and calm so that you can respond positively to events in your life. What you see in your mind's eye can strongly influence your beliefs and achievements. Our central nervous system does not distinguish between real and imagined events: It sees and accepts all images as if they were real. For example, close your eyes right now and imagine a juicy, sour lemon. In your mind, cut a big wedge from the lemon and place it in your mouth. Bite down, and let the sour juices permeate your entire mouth. Did you find yourself puckering or salivating?

—*Jerry Lynch and Chungliang Al Huang,* Thinking Body,
Dancing Mind

A Winter's (Golf) Tale

First I "see" the ball where I want it to finish,
nice and white and sitting up high on bright green
grass. Then the scene quickly changes and I "see"
the ball going there: its path, trajectory, and
shape, even its behavior on landing. Then there is
a sort of fade-out, and the next scene shows me
making the kind of swing that will turn the
previous images into reality.

—*Jack Nicklaus,* Golf My Way

WE WERE SITTING AT A SCARRED WOODEN TABLE AT
O'Rourke's Tavern in Driggs, Idaho—the Voodoo Hotdogs and I—wondering whether it might ever stop snowing.
Outside the frosted windows, a few inches of fluffy new powder had settled on my four-wheel-drive vehicle since I'd
parked it an hour earlier. The wind was blowing hard and the
streets were empty save for the occasional Jeep Cherokee or
Land Rover, ski rack full, wandering restlessly in the dark
night in search of a meal or a place to stay.

I hadn't exactly planned this stopover; actually, I'd never
even heard of Driggs, Idaho, until I was already in the middle
of it, having just come over the Teton Pass from Jackson,
Wyoming. The pass had been treacherous—near-whiteout
conditions kept me guessing which way the road turned,
and I could pick up only a single gospel station on my radio
for company. I was almost glad not to be able to see what
the drop-off to my left looked like, though the music more
than once led me to consider turning my wheel irrevocably
in that direction. Conditions were so bad that the Idaho
Highway Patrol closed the pass not long after I'd gotten
through.

Unfortunately, they also closed the road going out the other end of town. Just as I thought I was leaving Driggs behind forever in my rearview mirror, I came upon a police road-block—a "roadblock" in Idaho consisting of one corpulent officer sitting in his rig parked across the middle of the high-way, drinking coffee and reading a Stephen King novel.

I pulled up next to him and we rolled down our windows. "Road's closed," he said.

"Closed?" I asked. "The road's closed?" I repeated myself because nothing like this would ever have occurred to me. Then, like any New Yorker, I tried to bargain with the offi-cer, tried to elicit information on some secret alternative route that might take me toward my destination of Sun Valley, several hundred miles to the northwest. It didn't seem possible that a road could really be closed. And not just a road: *the* road.

The officer actually glanced up from his book for a fleeting moment—perhaps he'd just finished a chapter. "It's drifted over. You can't go anywhere. You're here for the night at least," he said, as if showing me to my cell in the county lockup. Then he shut his window and started reading again.

Back in Driggs, I was lucky to find a motel room and an open tavern; lucky, even, to find the Voodoo Hotdogs, a blues band trying to get home to Missoula, Montana, after playing a gig in Jackson the night before. The Dogs turned out to be fine dinner companions, and we had an excellent time writing lyrics for a new song about being stranded in a place not unlike Driggs, Idaho, in a snowstorm.

After the Dogs and I ordered yet another beer, and as the snow camouflaged the details of the world outside, the band's lead guitarist leaned across the table and held his Bud Light toward me like a microphone.

"If I may take the liberty of asking," he said, with great formality, "what brings you, sir, to Driggs on a wintry night like this?"

I tried to think of something clever, something funny, but all I came up with was the truth.

"I'm in the middle of a two-week golf outing," I said into the brown neck of the bottle, and the Hotdogs howled.

What is this true meditation? It is to make everything: coughing, swallowing, waving the arms, motion, still-ness, words, actions, the evil and the good, prosperity and shame, gain and loss, right and wrong, into one single koan.

—*Hakuin*

That winter I had contracted with a magazine to visit, eval-uate, and compare more than a dozen golf properties in the Rocky Mountain region, and to write a feature story describing the best of them. My editor originally intended to send me during June, when I might at least have seen the golf courses I'd be writing about. But as the magazine had promised all potential resort advertisers that a writer would definitely visit their properties with a view toward writing about them, when the publication date of this annual issue got pushed forward I found myself touring in the middle of February, during one of the most severe winters the Rockies have experienced since much of Colorado was trapped beneath a glacier 30,000 years ago. My journey would have inspired an excellent blues song.

In addition to driving through blizzards to fifteen resorts spread across Colorado, Wyoming, and Idaho in sixteen days, over the kinds of mountain roads that Camrys and Accords have nightmares about, the real challenge of my assignment was to visualize my destinations as if I'd visited them in July, when the golf courses would have stretched greenly beneath a clear blue sky and I might have ended each day sipping a cool drink by the swimming pool as a flaming sun dropped behind jagged peaks.

Many books about New Age or Eastern philosophies—particularly those that advocate applying their principles to sports, business, or personal life—recommend visualization as a meditative technique to help maximize performance. Such visualizations may involve, for example, picturing yourself winning the U.S. Open with a perfect one iron that sets up an eagle on the eighteenth hole at Baltusrol; or maybe seeing yourself delivering a sales presentation that inspires tears and concludes with a standing ovation from a tough audience. Whatever activity your visualization applies to, you can use the technique as a form of self-actualization: First you see yourself performing in a certain way, and then you perform the way you visualized yourself. Many golf instructors and tour players also suggest that meditating upon and visualizing good shots makes them more likely to occur. Visualization represents a sort of active Western version of more formal Eastern meditation.

In my particular circumstances, after speaking with resort pros and consulting press materials, scorecards, yardage guides, and photos, I needed—as the authors of *Thinking Body, Dancing Mind* advocate—to visualize far broader aspects of experience than a particular bunker shot or my approach to an elevated green. I needed to "tap inner sources of peace and calm so I could respond positively to events in my life." Which ideally required picturing every shot on each hole of fifteen different golf courses I'd never actually seen, imagining the kinds of swings that would launch my ball up against the backdrop of mountains and land it on the specific fairways I'd only read about. In theory, I had to fool my central nervous system into believing that these golf experiences I "saw" in my mind's eye were real, so as to write about them firsthand. Then I needed to visualize myself writing an excellent story as if I'd truly been to the places I was writing about.

This assignment presented me with a chance to practice a particularly extreme, multi-leveled, and slightly twisted version of meditative visualization. But I was certain that these strange circumstances also possessed a deeper, more subtle aspect—that they were trying to tell me something. I sensed that I'd been sent to the Rockies on a golf assignment in the middle of winter to satisfy a higher purpose. I believed that this bizarre mission must contain an essential lesson about golf—a lesson that the game couldn't teach me during the warmer months. By paring down the elements of this golfing trip, by eliminating everything familiar (including the golfing itself), this assignment presented another challenging golf koan that was even further beyond the fairway than golfing at night. If I studied it with a pure heart and a clear mind, it might reveal a sparkling new dimension of the game and expand my perceptions. I simply needed to discover exactly where the lesson lay concealed, and how to interpret its teachings.

Two assistant pros were walking the course early in the spring, when the grass was still muddy and full of large puddles. On the fairway of the eighth hole they came upon a beautiful young club member who could not get across an expanse of water.

"Come on, miss," said the first assistant pro. Lifting her in his arms, he carried her over the temporary pond.

The second assistant pro did not speak again until later that afternoon, when they were back in the pro shop. Then he could no longer restrain himself. "Assistant pros are not supposed to go near beautiful young club members," he said. "It's dangerous. Why did you do that?"

"I left the girl there," the first assistant pro replied. "Are you still carrying her?"

—Zen golf koan

Since I couldn't actually play any golf during my Rocky Mountain golf tour—or even look at the courses, which were buried under many feet of snow—and as there were several afternoons when I *didn't* have to drive 1,200 miles in bad weather, the only sensible thing left for me to do was go skiing. As I was already practicing a rather unusual form of visualization to write my golf story, this process was already on my mind. So I also applied it in a more conventional way.

The Purgatory Ski Area lies just down the road from what I visualized as Tamarron Resort's excellent golf course, and I headed there on a warm, sunny Colorado morning, after one storm had broken and the next had not yet rolled in. I skied a few warmup runs on the front side of the mountain, visualizing my own perfect form as I serpentined downhill, seeing myself leaning first one way and then the other in perfect rhythm and balance, reaching forward and planting my poles before pivoting around them. My weight remained centered perfectly over my boots. My knees flexed forward below my perfectly muscled thighs. In my mind's eye, I wore a black cowboy hat and dark Ray Bans.

After my warm-up on intermediate terrain, I headed for the black diamonds: steep, narrow trails crammed with moguls. As I gazed down one particularly harrowing run—searching for the mildest route through the bumps, a route that might allow me to hold on to my dental work and reach the bottom without grinding down the ball sockets in my joints—I felt a creeping sense of déjà vu.

That very morning, over breakfast, I'd been looking at a map and yardage guide to Tamarron's golf course and visualizing my own golf round along its dramatic fairways—the textbook backswings and follow-throughs, the way my ball landed on the grass and then released for an extra twenty yards, how my chips rolled up to within a couple feet of the holes. Now, as I followed the lines of this steep ski trail and used the same technique to visualize my run, it suddenly occurred to me that golf holes and ski runs share some striking similarities. Both are carved out of the surrounding terrain, receive careful grooming and manicuring, and present mostly clear, winding paths between trees and gullies and streams. Both golfing and skiing also involve interacting with the natural environment directly and on an individual basis by moving across and exploring the terrain. Even the basic objectives share a common idea: to stay between the borders and not wander out of bounds. Yet, at the same time, you can experience some of the best skiing and golfing moments by venturing off the trail or into the rough. As I hammered my knees in the steep bumps at Purgatory, I knew I'd found the key to my Rocky Mountain golf koan; visualization—which I'd first considered in terms of writing my story, then employed in my skiing, and ultimately realized was also a key to good golfing—was leading me in an unexpected direction. Once I realized that this personal, individualistic technique could help improve both my golf and my skiing, this led me to see much deeper connections between the two sports.

Picking my way between moguls, I let my body unconsciously bend and pivot down the slope while my mind pursued further links between skiing and golf. I noted, for example, that all the golf resorts I was visiting on this trip had transformed into ski resorts for the winter, and that this was also true nationwide, from Sun River, Oregon, to Stratton, Vermont. In many places, shops that sell golf equipment in summer metamorphose into ski shops when the weather turns cold.

As I bounced violently downhill and occasionally smashed myself in the chin with my own knees, further similarities flew into my head. Whereas golf courses often have three sets of color-coded tees to represent different levels of difficulty, ski mountains also mark the difficulty of trails with three colors. Both sports require you to buy a ticket, which you're supposed to display as proof you've paid your fee. In both sports you ride to the beginning of each hole or trail by mechanical means, whether cart or chairlift. And eighteen runs make for a full day of skiing.

I dropped down to where a flatter, easier trail intersected the mogul run and slowed my pace, thighs burning, lungs gasping to suck a little oxygen out of the cold, thin air. It seemed so obvious to me how golf and skiing complement each other—summer yin and winter yang—to compose a harmonic, individualistic sporting whole. By pursuing both in their seasons, one could achieve perfect balance. But the parallels run far deeper than merely superficial coincidences. In the course of skiing at a few other golf resorts on my itinerary, I recognized that the connections between golf and skiing extend beyond the outward fairways and slopes to the very unmanicured—or ungroomed—hearts of both of these pristine, aesthetic, and individualistic sports.

He who knows others is wise
He who knows himself is enlightened.
—Tao Te Ching

Snowmass Lodge's Ken Everett is one of several Colorado golf pros who claim to ski as well as they golf. The fact that Everett holds the resort's course record (65) says a lot about his downhill technique. During the winter Everett organizes a snow-golf tournament for local club members, and also runs a weekly ski-with-the-golf-pro program, establishing an intrinsic connection between the two sports—a connection I wasn't the first person to recognize, but one that I fully expected would reveal something to me.

During my visit, Everett took me right out to the golf shop, which was outfitted with cross-country ski gear for winter, and set me up with the necessary equipment for touring the golf course at that time of year. A few minutes later we were gliding across the snow-covered fairways, where I could feel the humps and bumps beneath my feet and experience the links in a brand-new way—sort of like reading them in Braille. Cross-country skiing often takes place on golf courses across the northern part of the globe, and you can't connect the two sports more directly than pursuing them on the exact same terrain, especially as the very object of each sport is to move across that terrain. But more important, skiing, like the highest level of golf, has no destination; the activity is its own goal, and you journey toward it at your own pace and in your own way.

I'd never been strapped to cross-country skis before, so I followed Everett slowly and clumsily (much as I might have if we'd been golfing) up and down the contours of the course as he described the holes, pointing out creeks and bunkers, where doglegs turned, and how some of the greens played. I'd never been much interested in Nordic skiing before; given a chance, I always headed for the downhill slopes, eschewing what I perceived as the slow, lumbering effort required to scramble across flattish ground. But this was different from how I'd imagined it. I found myself relating very closely to the terrain in a sort of moving meditation, a rhythm that seemed to link my breathing and body motions to something far larger than myself. When Everett and I finished eighteen holes and found ourselves back near the putting green, I told him to go on in without me, I wanted to ski a little more. He pointed me across the road to where the golf course ended and a few other trails disappeared into a valley.

As soon as I traveled across the road and out of sight of the pro shop, I realized that I was literally *skiing* beyond the fairway, and the idea greatly appealed to me because of everything I believe about such movement into unmanicured terrain. I stopped worrying about where I was going. I stopped concentrating on my form, on pushing off with the left arm and the right ski, the right arm and left ski, on springing and gliding the way Everett had instructed me. I transcended such thoughts, realizing that, much like the golf swing, this kind of skiing was all form, but that reaction worked better than reflection, and if I could switch off my analytical side I'd more thoroughly enjoy myself. I simply visualized myself skiing the way I'd seen Olympians skiing on TV.

At some point during the late afternoon, as I reemerged from an elegant aspen and pine grove, it occurred to me that cross-country skiing was also a bit like visiting the driving range: You could make your own tracks and wander widely through the sport's terrain without worrying about straying too far off-line. And if you made a mistake and took a fall, it in no way ruined the experience, because—just as with the purest Scottish golf—it was the process, the journey that mattered, and there was no need to keep score.

> If the waves of the Zen stream were all alike, innumerable ordinary people would get bogged down.
> —*Zen saying*

A few days later, while visiting the Teton Pines resort, in Jackson, Wyoming, I was lucky enough to hit more horrendous weather—which forced me to stay an extra day. I was also fortunate enough to go both cross-country and downhill skiing with the resort's amicable assistant golf pro and public relations director, Jeff Heilbrun, who excelled at both sports.

On my first afternoon in Jackson, Heilbrun Nordic-skied me across the golf course for an hour, and then suggested that we head up to an old logging road he knew, where the powder would be untracked and the terrain a bit wilder. We spent a couple of hours frolicking in the snow and talking about golf. I asked Heilbrun if he had any insight into this strange ski-golf connection I'd discovered, and without having to give it much thought, he rattled off a number of similarities between the

119

two sports. On the surface, he said, both sports were "singular-color activities. In golf, everything is green, and in skiing it's all white.

"Also, you can't think about each individual move in skiing or in golf," Heilbrun added, supporting the notion that had occurred to me at Snowmass. "You can't think, 'Weight left, bend this knee,' because you'll just tumble down the slope. It must be a free-flowing thing; you can't clutter your mind. Just like in golf—you'd be OB and over a cliff somewhere." In the style of the most learned Masters, Heilbrun talked about an essential aspect of Eastern philosophy—transcendence—without explicitly naming it.

Speaking of cliffs, my host took me out on a couple the following day. Although I was scheduled to leave in the morning for Sun Valley, two feet of new powder fell overnight, and Heilbrun promised to write a note from my mother excusing me if I decided to play hooky and spend the day downhill skiing with him on Jackson's most excellent mountain. When he finished twisting my arm, we headed off for a hot breakfast and the even hotter slopes.

I virtually had to plead with Heilbrun to let me take a warmup run on a groomed trail; he was that excited to get out to the unmanicured backcountry terrain, which he knew would be overfull with fresh snow. Which reminded me of fighting similar battles with my golfing companions whenever I insist on hitting a bucket of practice balls before heading for the number-one tee.

On that first groomed run (called Gros Ventre), I suddenly unraveled a major knot of the winter golf koan and understood—directly, not intellectually—what it means to "be the ball." Both golf and skiing involve movement down a carved path, but in golf, we travel by knocking a ball along the fairway and then following where it goes. In skiing, we drive *ourselves* along; we finally *are* the ball. I reveled in the speed and momentum of flying down that steep slope.

As we headed back to the chairlift there wasn't much time for philosophizing further. The Lower Faces were waiting: Cheyenne Bowl, the Hobacks, Riverton Bowl—steep, wide, open, off-trail terrain where every now and then a head popped out of the snow just long enough to scream "Yeeee-haw!" before disappearing again in a burst of airy powder. Heilbrun was like a bull out of the rodeo gate, and he dropped down the slope as if he were falling through clouds. Occasionally his black mustache rose to the surface before his body pulled it under again. When he was permanently gone from sight, I visualized the perfect powder run: how I would disappear in bursts of fluffy snow and then reappear briefly, rising out of my turns, before descending out of sight again; I envisioned how my tracks—if viewed from a helicopter—would carve immaculate "S"'s in the snow. I pushed off with my poles and abandoned myself to gravity, to the unrestrained adrenaline rush of acceleration, without worrying about how I looked, what it meant, where it might lead. Because I just goddamned well felt like it.

By three o'clock that afternoon, my legs felt like bags of wet cement, and we had to retreat to the Mangy Moose Saloon for a couple of beers. Drinking icy drafts on a cushioned stool and watching certain pairs of stretch pants slink by, I realized one more great similarity between golfing and skiing. Heilbrun and I were sitting in the bar with that good tiredness exactly as if we were golfers lounging around the nineteenth hole; we leaned back into our fatigue while the heat returned to our faces, and we tried to relive every moment we'd spent outside moving like flowing water across the sport's terrain. And we talked about other challenging ground we'd covered both skiing and golfing, the difficulties of which were measured by steep slopes and steep slope ratings.

One rainy day, the greenskeeper was lying on a couch out in his office adjacent to the equipment shed, reading a Zen golf book. One of the caddies saw him and said, "Greenskeeper! You must maintain dignity when reading a Zen golf book."
The greenskeeper raised up one leg.
The caddy had nothing to say.

—Zen golf koan

It's easy to visualize your performance in sports such as golfing and skiing because so much of their action occurs individually, without interruption by an opponent trying to thwart your perfect motion, or even by a teammate. In a team sport such as football it would be far tougher to visualize making the perfect touchdown reception both because the pass itself might not be perfect (no matter how well you visualize it) since it originates with another person, and because a defender might stick his hand in your face at the last moment, altering the way you'd envisioned the scene. In sports such as golf and skiing, you can concentrate simply on your own performance without worrying about such outside variables.

Visualizing—itself a personal, individualistic activity—would seem to work best in precisely such individualistic sports as skiing and golf. In fact, other sports to which visu-

122

alization easily applies—such as kayaking, rock climbing, biking, running, surfing, and scuba diving (what a friend of mine calls the "I-N-G adventure sports") are also purely individualistic activities that an athlete pursues alone.

Although in some ways Eastern philosophy and individualism seem contradictory because, for example, the latter may involve some degree of ego attachment, Zen still requires each practitioner to pursue his own path, to come to terms with an ultimate personal reality, to aim at knowing himself. By offering no particular doctrine or dogma and requiring no specific rituals, Zen expresses the same individualistic nature as do these sports. While koan study and meditation provide excellent and traditional vehicles by which to pursue enlightenment, we might as easily attain a higher state of consciousness by taking up archery or cooking, painting or motorcycle maintenance, skiing or golf. The Masters instruct us to seek higher states through every task of our everyday lives. Ultimately, regardless of the path we choose to move along, we must undertake the journey alone. Among the great many potential routes toward enlightenment, golf and skiing offer a couple of particularly individualistic and transcendent ways.

Because the trip to enlightenment is individual and the paths many and varied, seekers may vary widely and weirdly. Those whose perceptions of the world are fresh, expansive, quirky, or sometimes even downright bizarre may themselves seem pretty strange to others whose roads lead another way. But, eventually, all individual roads converge in the great Oneness that lies beyond the fairway.

CHAPTER EIGHT

Golfing to Extremes

The thing about Zen is that it pushes
contradictions to their ultimate limit where one
has to choose between madness and innocence.
And Zen suggests that we may be driving toward
one or the other on a cosmic scale.
—*Thomas Merton*, Zen and the Birds of Appetite

Sometimes people who emerge from nirvana
precipitately . . . become mentally unstable or
even deranged. This is one source of the
eccentricity known in technical literature as
"crazy Zen."
—*Thomas Cleary*, No Barrier: Unlocking the Zen Koan

WHEN JACK STALLINGS LOOKS OUT THE BACK DOOR OF the clubhouse at the Northstar Golf Course in Fairbanks, Alaska, he sees plush emerald fairways stretching across a sylvan valley at the foot of wild, rugged mountains. He sees raised tee boxes floating like lush islands above the thick, rolling grass. He sees contoured, undulating greens as soft and lovely as a woman's face. He sees a perfectly groomed layout carved—rescued, even—from a relentless wilderness virtually on the edge of the Arctic Circle, an impossibly impractical yet nonetheless miraculous golf venue at the very outer edges of the middle of nowhere. Perhaps it's no exaggeration to say that Stallings sees the Augusta National of the Yukon—an exquisite, challenging Scottish-style golf course set within the most unmanicured, beyond-the-fairway terrain in North America.

What most everyone else sees when they visit Northstar Golf Course is a potato field where somebody pushed around just enough dirt so that you can't even grow potatoes anymore. They see a mosquito-infested swamp with a few roughly shorn fairways cut into the land like clumsy Mohawk haircuts.

I had the opportunity to experience Northstar (to say that I played there would be taking far too much literary license) just two days after Stallings officially opened his self-designed, self-financed, and largely self-constructed layout—a monument to both individualism and creative visualization. Accompanying me was Dave Curwen, president of the Fairbanks Golf Association and one of more than a hundred locals who supposedly paid several hundred dollars in advance for membership in this new club.

Jack Stallings couldn't join us during our round because

he had to work the desk in the pro shop—a duty which on that day turned out to be unnecessary, as no other golfers showed up. But he did offer some advice as Curwen and I picked up a scorecard and headed out to play. First, Stallings provided basic directions on how to find our way from hole to hole; then he encouraged us in his friendly, avuncular manner simply to take a free drop if we lost any balls in the middle of fairways. He said this deadpan, without a trace of sarcasm. "Things are still a little rough out there," he explained, and Curwen and I foolishly took this bit of prophecy in stride.

In retrospect, of course, I see that Stallings' words should have served as a warning, but I was too excited to be heading out on a virtually unplayed golf course, too busy fantasizing about setting a new course record that might stand for hours, if not days, to pay much attention to what he said. I should have remembered where I was, remembered that in Alaska, crazy dreams are the state bird, and little happens as you expect it to. Still, it's probably safe to say that nothing could have fully prepared me for golfing Northstar.

Out on the first tee, Curwen and I doused ourselves with jungle-formula insect repellent—noting meanwhile that we were then in the most drained and developed section of the golf course—and gazed out over the nine-hole layout and beyond, to where the land for the back nine had already been cleared. From this small promontory on a high edge of the valley, we could see fairways winding languidly through an ocean of tall grass and yellow flags poking up occasionally like the sails of lonely boats. From where we stood, it truly looked like a golf course, and a dramatic one, at that. Snow-capped mountains ringed the valley on every side, pressing up against the cool, gray Alaskan sky. Wild animals lived in those mountains, I knew; every golfer in the state could tell you stories about how a moose had once attacked the flag, or how an eagle had dived and carried off his partner's lucky hat, or how a grizzly had eaten the leg of a member of another foursome as the guy was lining up a birdie putt, which he sank anyway.

Both Curwen and I hit respectable drives on number one, out into a flat where the hole began curving around a truly dangerous waste area. But after climbing over a fallen tree and skirting some black standing water in the fairway, we couldn't find either ball. We eventually took free drops and kept our thoughts to ourselves. Perhaps, like me, Curwen was figuring that this first hole must be an aberration, and that conditions would surely improve. A five handicap who'll be retiring from the Fairbanks police force shortly to pursue a career in golf, Dave Curwen is no wimp, and I just assumed that as an Alaskan he was accustomed to playing on golf courses where you couldn't see your shoes through the thick grass—on the fairway. I assumed that the shifting clouds of buzzing skeeters had no effect on his concentration. But when we finished the initial hole and then spent ten minutes trying to decipher where the next tee was, this stoic homicide detective turned to me and confessed, "I'm not going to make it."

We played the next couple of holes in stunned silence, but by number four, Curwen apparently decided to adopt a different approach: optimism. I admired his effort.

"I think I'm beginning to see a layout," he admitted, trying to convince himself that the membership dues he'd paid were not completely ill-spent and conditions weren't as bad as they seemed, but, of course, they were.

By the fifth hole, after losing a few more balls and nearly losing his golf shoes to the sucking mud when he ventured into the fringe to search for an errant shot, Curwen turned cynical. He remarked that the fairways looked a lot like U.S. Open rough, which made them quite playable compared to the rough, which he didn't even dare to comment upon. As we moved slowly along the seemingly interminable fifth, dropping balls on every shot, Curwen and I began to discuss a truly frightening prospect: that Jack Stallings, a nice man who would never consciously try to mislead anybody, actually imagined there was a golf course out there.

I consulted my scorecard for a moment, as if that might somehow reassure me.

In fact, the card looked like the kind you'd get at any public golf course, printed in red, green, blue, and gold, with ads for insurance agencies, banks, car dealerships, and local restaurants. It provided all the essential information for an eighteen-hole, par-72 golf course of 6,652 yards from the blue tees. It had empty boxes for all the members of a foursome to write their names and scores for each hole. It gave yardages, pars, and handicaps. Looking at that carefully designed, perfectly believable scorecard, I understood implicitly that when Jack Stallings ordered hundreds of these from the printer, he did so with the unshakable faith that the golf course described on it really and truly existed in the bog through which Dave Curwen and I were slogging. In what must have been a truly remarkable example of visualization,

Stallings had created—albeit in his own mind and possibly in the same way I imagined that I'd played fifteen golf courses in the Rocky Mountains, though I'd visited them in winter—a well-tended golf course out of this expanse of muddy, overgrown land.

Discussing visualization, the authors of *Thinking Body, Dancing Mind* write, "Our central nervous system does not distinguish between real and imagined events. It sees and accepts all images as if they were real." As I learned at Northstar, Jack Stallings makes no such distinctions, either.

But I also came to understand something far more important: that Jack Stallings's vision of a Northstar Golf Course full of happy players riding around in motorized carts, unzipping symmetrical, sod-bottomed divots with crisp iron shots, and sipping gin drinks on the veranda of his clubhouse as if it were a Sunday in July at the Westchester Country Club is not so different from the spirit of dreaming that's endemic to the game of golf—not only in Alaska, where extremes are the norm and the terrain is all unmanicured, but everywhere that men and women tramp along in the grass and hit a ball with a stick.

Stallings's particular golf vision isn't much different in spirit from that of a twenty-eight handicapper who steps up on the first tee at his local course and addresses his ball, thinking, "Today is the day I break par," and actually visualizes himself hitting all the right shots, truly sees himself entering 3's and 4's on his scorecard—before slicing two drives so deep into the woods that the balls will biodegrade before anyone finds them. But then a few minutes later, after carding a 7X on number one, that same player climbs up on the second tee and thinks, "Okay, now I know what I've been doing wrong.

If I just close my stance a little, it's not too late to break 80"—although he's never broken 80 and probably never will. He visualizes a long, straight, towering drive unlike any he's ever hit (or is likely to hit) in his life, before topping his tee shot barely past the ladies' tee.

At its very core, golf is about dreams and visions and aspirations, and every game—every hole, even every shot—presents a chance to make the most elusive and unlikely of these real. We play golf always hoping that today might be the day when we execute a chain of perfect shots linked together into a spectacular round, that for just a few hours out of an entire lifetime we might become untouchable, immaculate, enlightened, that we might realize fully and without self-consciousness the most minuscule details of that most improbable dream. The least we can do is envision this, even if we're unable to make it come true.

The very same spirit that inspires unremarkable players to dare imagine an unforgettable round also sparks a seventy-four-year-old Alaskan individualist to dream a golf course out of a swamp. This spirit, more than anything, is why we play the game.

In his book *The Songlines,* Bruce Chatwin writes about Australian Aborigines who cannot recognize geographic features without first singing them into existence. Throughout the world, golfers perform the same kind of ritual by dreaming into existence perfect chip shots, low scores, or new swings. Some golf instructors, New Age mystics, or modern-day Eastern philosophers might call this imaging or visualization, but in essence they are talking about dreaming—the very substance of golf. From one perspective, visualization *is* dreaming, and without dreams, without the hope at every moment of flawlessness or something infinitesimally close to it, we wouldn't be obsessed with the game. We wouldn't fantasize about it at work, wouldn't anticipate our next round with the excitement usually reserved for meeting a new lover. We would not erect nets in the backyard or pitch balls at the water fountain in the park until the light fades and the shadows fall. We would not care to celebrate even the briefest moments of clarity and beauty and impeccable form. Golfing, too, *is* dreaming—about everything that we haven't accomplished yet, everything that is imminently possible but hasn't quite come to pass, whether enlightenment, mastery of an apparently simple game, both simultaneously, or something different altogether. But golfing is also an effort to make those dreams come true. And that is why in places such as Alaska, which seem so far from the fairway—*especially* in places such as Alaska, a last frontier where anything is still possible—the game means so much, and its players dream it and pursue that dream with such power and intensity. Jack Stallings visualizes the Northstar Golf Course to try and make it real.

When we finished the sixth hole, Dave Curwen and I agreed to risk cutting across knee-deep rough, through battalions of mosquitoes, toward where we guessed the ninth tee might be, modestly hoping only to make it back to the clubhouse intact. Which didn't seem like much to expect from a round of golf. As we struggled over a route appropriate to an Outward Bound course, Curwen turned reflective.

"You know, if you came out here and forgot your mosquito repellent, and had to run cross-country back to your car, they'd probably never find your body." Then he paused for a moment and slapped at a few low-flying insects before adding, "I was talking to a defendant last night when I was on duty . . . trying to get some information out of him. I should have just brought the guy out here for a while."

We played the ninth hole hurriedly, although Curwen grew suddenly intent on parring it, even though you couldn't putt—could barely *chip*—on the green. And then it was over: We'd survived every danger of the Northstar Golf Course, and I had only a few questions for Jack Stallings before my day was complete and I could drive way too fast in my rental car on the gravel roads that led out of there.

Was this arrogance, or was it more perhaps an expression of the absolute freedom he had achieved?
—*Perle Besserman and Manfred Steger,*
Crazy Clouds: Zen Radicals, Rebels, and Reformers

A disciple asked the Head Pro, "Speech and silence involve alienation and vagueness; how does one get through without transgression?"

The Head Pro said, "I always remember the lake south of the ninth hole in springtime, the hundred flowers fragrant where the partridges call."
—*Zen golf koan*

Inside the clubhouse, Stallings brought me a cup of bitter coffee in a paper cup and bought Dave Curwen a beer because it was his birthday. He is a gentle, soft-spoken, eminently likable man, Jack Stallings is, though given to long, rambling tangents. He began our conversation by admitting that the golf course still needed some work, but then he described how the greens and tees would be completed down to the finishing touches in a couple more weeks. I wondered if he realized that there actually *weren't* any tees or greens to speak of, but as he continued it became even more obvious that this man saw something that I didn't have the vision or the proper dream channel or the specific requisite dysfunction to see for myself.

Because Zen is a naturally individualistic pursuit and because enlightenment involves creative perception, over the centuries a few monks developed paths that were so uniquely quirky and outlandish they were considered to represent almost a separate branch of Zen: Rinzai, for example, who grabbed and insulted priests, government officials, and the social elite to shock them into enlightenment; Bassui, who moved into a tree house following official confirmation of his enlightenment and refused to teach; and Hakuin, who broke all the rules by accepting women and peasants as his students. Called Crazy Clouds, these often-misunderstood individualists were actually true geniuses—so ingenious that even other practitioners couldn't always comprehend the depth and creativity of their Zen learning.

I listened politely to Jack Stallings for about forty-five minutes. Occasionally I'd ask a question—how many members did the Northstar Golf Club have, for example—and Stallings would gallop off along a completely different line of thought, such as the Japanese tourists who visit Fairbanks and want to play golf. By far the most alarming aspect of our conversation came during a few brief moments when I actually began to see Northstar the way Stallings did, my misgivings about his consistent lucidity notwithstanding. I had trouble determining what really sounded plausible because I'd been in Alaska for three days by then, and as it hadn't ever gotten dark yet, I hadn't really gone to sleep. Let's just say that he displayed flashes of total rationality, and at some point toward the end of our conversation it occurred to me that in the manner of the great Zen Crazy Clouds and other spiritual Masters, perhaps Jack Stallings had completely transcended subjective reality, that in some way his visualization had succeeded, that he might, indeed, be living in a state of satori and continuous revelation.

A monk once asked a Zen Master, "What is Buddha?"

The Master, in a pure display of his Zen learning, answered, "Three pounds of burlap."

If you hit a ball along a swath of once-mowed grass, does this constitute a golf course?

Sometimes you must ponder the simplest questions for the longest time to understand their implications. Sometimes you can't see the obvious until you step beyond the manicured logic of rational thought. Jack Stallings: mystic or maniac? Irredeemable dreamer lost in maya, or a visionary who created a Northstar golf koan that only the purest mind can unravel?

As the Head Pro was entering handicaps into the computer early on a summer evening, one of his potential successors stood in front of the counter in the pro shop, cut off his own arm, and said, "My mind is not yet at peace. Please pacify my mind."

The Head Pro said, "Bring me your mind, and I will pacify it for you."

134

The potential successor said, "I have looked for my mind, and cannot find it."

The Head Pro said, "I have pacified your mind for you."

—*Zen golf koan*

However history or the Fairbanks Golf Association ultimately judges Jack Stallings, the fact is that such twisted personal visions as his seem to thrive in Alaska, the land of midnight sun and noontime darkness, the topography and terrain of dreamers. Dreaming is an essential element of survival in a country where winter temperatures regularly drop below zero and the sun may *not* come up tomorrow. How else could one persevere through prolonged twilight and darkness than to make love, read books, drink good whiskey, and dream shimmering visions of summer? And how better to dream summer than through images of golfing long into the warm, sleepless, never-dark nights?

Two days after the summer solstice—when the sun skipped along the horizon line without ever dropping below it, and a sort of seven o'clock pre-dusk filled the sky long past midnight—a sign scribbled on a chalkboard outside the men's locker room at Settler's Bay Golf Course, in Wasilla, read: "Golf hard. The days are getting shorter." Which is precisely why many Alaskans play golf until eleven or twelve every summer night, compressing a full year of rounds into June, July, and August. In response to the inevitable winter, they pursue long-nurtured dreams when they can, and golf fast and hard, for tomorrow it will grow dark, and someday we will die. That Alaskans not only play golf amidst the tundra and permafrost, but they endure the most bizarre conditions, the greatest hardships, and still love the game with a degree of passion that matches their patent weirdness, attests to the fact that this far from the fairway, the game takes on deeper context, greater meaning. Golf provides a way for Alaskans to assert that they are still alive.

All of which brings up the case of Tim Ellingwood.

While I was examining my lie on the fairway of the tenth hole at Moose Run Golf Course, just north of Anchorage, halfway into my Alaskan golf journey, one of the players in my foursome pointed back toward the parking lot and said, "Hey. There's Tim Ellingwood. Let's see if he wants to play along." Since our group was composed of one of the resident teaching pros, the head greenskeeper, myself, and Jim Colell (a friend I'd made earlier that same day on another golf course), and since it was also nearly ten P.M., adding a fifth to our group wasn't a problem. The teaching pro gunned his cart back toward the parking lot (pros in Alaska all drive carts on which the governors have been removed, so they run like squat Indy cars) while the rest of us hit into the tenth green.

A few minutes later, on the eleventh tee, I got my first glimpse of Tim Ellingwood, a soft-spoken, handsome man in his thirties who hobbled from the cart wearing a neck brace, a back brace, an elbow brace, and two wrist braces. As Ellingwood limped over and then struggled to bend down and tee up his ball, the pro whispered that Tim had been in a pretty nasty car wreck only a few days after taking his clubs out for the season (one way they measure time in Alaska), which meant about three weeks before.

Although at that very moment he probably should have

been hooked up to an IV at a local hospital, the undeniable facts were that (1) it was June in Alaska; (2) in another two weeks Ellingwood would have to defend his title as the state amateur champion; and (3) most obviously, the golf season wouldn't last forever. Too soon, there would be only the dreams, so Ellingwood may very well have sneaked out of intensive care to squeeze in a few leisurely holes. To live in the moment.

Just before Ellingwood addressed his ball, George Collum, the teaching pro and a longtime adversary of Tim's, asked how his rehabilitation was going, and Ellingwood described how that very day he'd been stuck with twenty-five needles. On hearing this detail, Jim Colell—a six handicap with an innate understanding of the golf swing—said, "I press." Then Ellingwood uncoiled a 270-yard drive and shuffled back to the cart.

It was nearly one A.M. before we finished the round at Moose Run. In fact, during almost two weeks of golfing my way around America's last frontier, I played golf until midnight or later almost every day. I did so because it allowed me to laugh in the face of time, to use the planet's spin to my personal advantage, and most simply because I could. When I drove out of the parking lot at Moose Run that night on my way home, a maintenance worker was motoring around the golf course on his tractor at one A.M. Down the street a woman pulled weeds from her garden. Children flew past on bikes. It was so completely surreal that I wanted to roll down my car window and scream, "*Go to sleep! Don't you people know it's the middle of the night?*" But these were Alaskans, dreaming their world of sunlight and pursuing it while they could, before darkness fell.

There is an order of Buddhist monks in Japan whose practice is running. They are called the marathon monks of Mount Hiei. They begin running at one-thirty A.M. and run from eighteen to twenty-five miles per night, covering several of Mount Hiei's most treacherous slopes. Because of the high altitude, Mount Hiei has long cold winters and part of the mountain is called the Slope of Instant Sobriety; because it is so cold, it penetrates any kind of illusion or intoxication. The monks run all year round. They do not adjust their running schedule to the snow, wind, or ice. They wear white robes when they run, rather than the traditional Buddhist black. White is the color of death. There is always the chance of dying on the way. In fact, when they run they carry with them a sheathed knife and a rope to remind them to take their life by disembowelment or hanging if they fail to complete their route.

—*Natalie Goldberg,* Long Quiet Highway

Unmanicured golf happens as a matter of course during summers in the frozen north, before the bleak season of only-dreaming settles in again. But in a state known for zealots and hard-core individualists, serial killers, and a governor named Wally, there exists a small cadre of dangerous and demented local golfers who aren't content simply to dream their golf through the winter; they insist on playing in spite of the conditions. They make guys such as Tim Ellingwood look like wimps. While I felt, in Colorado, that I had to visualize my golf because it was winter, a group of Alaskan golfers make no such concessions to the season.

In fact, during the Alaskan summer, the golf course that hosts the annual Nome Ice Classic (played in February) doesn't even exist. By June it's already melted back into the ocean. But every winter, when most sensible Alaskans are either dreaming their golf adventures from a cozy seat by the wood stove or pursuing them in Arizona, nature re-creates a six-hole, par-three layout by freezing a section of the Bering Sea. In recent years, greenskeepers for the Ice Classic have imported sand traps to the ice floe links and drilled holes in the frozen surface so they could install a few trees. Elliot Staples, a tournament official, advises that serious contenders for this championship had better hit every green in regulation. "You'll never win if you wander off in the pressure ridges," he says, referring to a hazard most "lower-48" golfers needn't worry about.

Players at Nome tee up on empty shotgun shells (to simulate a shotgun start), and discuss course conditions with deep seriousness. Recently, golfers from Kodiak swept the competition, and local experts attributed this to the deep snow, a condition that is usually prevalent on Kodiak links; Nome golfers are more accustomed to playing on glass ice.

Not to be outdone by their rivals, Kodiak golfers also host their own off-season event. The annual Pillar Mountain Golf Classic provides another outlet for Alaskans who aren't content just to dream their golf during the cold, dark months. The Pillar Mountain tourney adheres to accepted PGA rules, with the following additions and amendments:

1. Devastating weather may postpone play one week.
2. No two-way radios, dogs, or guns allowed.

139

3. Don't saw down spruce trees or power poles.
4. Cursing golf officials carries a twenty-five-dollar fine.

If the rules seem unusual, they're nothing compared to the course—a par-70, 2,000-yard, one-hole layout which climbs 1,400 vertical feet up Pillar Mountain. The "fairway" consists of a rocky, snow-covered, abandoned four-wheel-drive road lined by alder thickets and a deep ravine. Before a recent tour event here (players claim membership in the Professional Cross-Country Golfer's Association, or PCCGA), the course was described as "treacherous, fast, and life-threatening." As at Scottish links courses such as Turnberry and Carnoustie, weather plays an important role at Pillar Mountain: Winds may reach 100 mph around the green, and temperatures often drop well below zero.

Warren Good, a winner at the first Pillar Mountain tournament in 1985, recommends a slightly unorthodox strategy to win this event: Send a spotter ahead of you on the course and aim at him. The key to victory is consistently finding your ball in deep snow. Golfers may employ a spotter and a caddy, and the team can use hatchets, hand saws (but no chain saws), and shovels to locate a ball and ensure a clear shot. The course record is 25, or 45 under par. The tournament began as a bar bet, but now raises money for local charities, including a hypothermia clinic.

Such is golf in Alaska, the most beautifully unmanicured of terrains, where golf dreams are enough to carry most (but not all) locals through the long, encompassing winters. Where winds howl and wolves call, and where it's essential to remember that no matter how bad things may seem at any particular moment—whether you've just hit three drives into a water hazard and the fourth into the sand, or it's the first of January and you haven't seen the sun in weeks—there's always another golf hole and always another season. All you need do is dream yourself through the present—or golf through it, if you're not prone to frostbite.

PART THREE

Into the Rough: Students, Masters, and Other Zen Golf Individualists

CHAPTER NINE

Fathers and Sons

So Agatha spoke about golf and about the love
men have for one another.

"It's the only reason ye play at all," she said.
"It's a way ye've found to get togither and yet
maintain a proper distance. I know you men.
Yer not like women or Italians huggin' and
embracin' each other. Ye need tae feel yer
separate love. Just look—ye winna' come home
on time if yer with the boys, I've learned that
o'er the years. The love ye feel for your friends
is too strong for that. All those gentlemanly
rools, why, they're the proper rools of
affection—all the waitin' and oohin' and ahin'
o'er yer shots, all the talk o' this one's drive
and that one's putt and the other one's gorgeous
swing—what is it all but love? Men lovin' men,
that's what golf is."

—*Michael Murphy,* Golf in the Kingdom

BEYOND THE FAIRWAY

The Wild Man, who has examined his wound,
resembles a Zen priest, a shaman, or a woodsman
more than a savage.
                                    —*Robert Bly,* Iron John

WE ARE ON THE SEVENTH HOLE OF GRAND VIEW LODGE'S
Pines Golf Course in the north woods of Minnesota in
early summer, my father and I. The day is perfect, the sky
blue, the air clean and crisp as a fine chardonnay.

The seventh hole is 150 yards from the back tees, all carry
over a lake. Beyond the slate-black surface of the water, a
small, undulating, bowl-shaped green warms in the afternoon
sun.

I tee off first from the blues and hit a lofting eight iron that
hangs in the denim sky for the longest time before finally
dropping with a satisfying *thunk* onto the soft grass on the back
of the green, thirty feet from the pin. I try my best not to
look too pleased.

My father approaches the white tees—ten yards closer—
with a seven wood. His yellow windbreaker stretches tightly
across his broad shoulders, but a great stiffness displays itself,
too, as he takes a cursory practice swipe. Over the years,
arthritis has narrowed the range of my father's swing, eclipsing
its power. I have trouble imagining him as the star running
back on his high school football team back in Brooklyn, in the
days when the Dodgers still played nearby. But he's got a
scrapbook to prove it, and it's become a sort of continuous
joke in our family that every girl I've ever brought home has,
with my surreptitious encouragement, asked to see the yel-
lowed clippings that he's still so proud of after half a century—
and that I am proud of, too.

My father maneuvers the heel of the club between his strong hands and plants his feet. He is not playing well today, but seems happy just to be out here beneath the fragrant pines.

He draws the club back slowly, with great precision, but as he begins his downswing his left shoulder drops too much and he begins to back away from the ball even as his clubhead advances to meet it. I recognize that he's about to knock this shot into the water. I anticipate the splash, his mild expletive, the way my dad will smile grimly and shrug his shoulders, as if he'd inadvertently burped at the table.

Of course, I watch anyway. I listen to the *ping* of metal wood against ball and see the low-trajectory shot barely skim above the surface of the water like a hydroplane, like a bomber on a low strafing mission, like a crop duster nearly dragging its wheels in the corn, before eventually, somehow, curling onto the green and breaking toward the hole. It wasn't pretty, but he's knocked it fifteen feet from the flag stick, half as close as my ball. He grins so completely—as if he'd *meant* to hit this particular shot—that his whole face reddens and expands, and I think he might dance a jig right there in the tee box. But he just bows instead, doffing the novelty hat that always embarrasses me—it is white, the visor splattered with greenish blobs of plastic meant to represent bird droppings, and emblazoned with the words I HATE SEA GULLS.

To anyone who happens to see us today, we must appear simply as a father and son out enjoying a round of golf together, cheering each other's good shots, ruing the bad ones. Earlier, when I mishit a long iron on the second hole, my dad whispered, "Keep your head down," as fathers have whispered to their sons for centuries, whether or not lifting heads had anything to do with why the sons' shots went awry. This

147

is a piece of advice—like saying "Be careful" when they hand over the car keys—that human evolution has genetically imprinted upon paternal DNA.

But beyond this obvious fairway view of a father and son sharing a leisurely pastime, of acting out our respective roles in an ancient ritual, far more is going on amid the pines and wildflowers on this summery midwestern day. Something else is occurring between us that demonstrates how much deeper and wider than the fairway the game of golf extends.

Many men of my generation share a common disappointment that our fathers were always, and continue to be, unreachable; while their advice (if they ever provide any) regarding power tools and mutual funds might be helpful, when it comes to relationships, illness, or any other more emotional subject, the men who helped raise us often have nothing to say. Perhaps, burdened with traditional and now outmoded views of the family—that a father must simply work hard and provide for his family's material comforts—our dads failed to recognize that what we really needed from them was so much simpler: an hour to toss a ball back and forth in the yard, an opportunity (even one disguised by the ritual of sport) to stand around and talk. That we craved at least a glimpse of what they were like on the inside, beyond their beard stubble, the scents of tobacco and cologne, and the crisp twenties from their wallets. That we wished only to know what they were thinking and feeling, to hear that they were scared sometimes, or felt pain, or worried about making it in the world. To see the vulnerability that, when my generation became men, we realized must have been there in our dads all along. To receive the wisdom of their age and experience and even their mistakes, to hear about their triumphs and regrets, rather than always watching them act strong and remain silent in the face of responsibility, suffering, and even death. To have a mentor whom we could emulate as we grew toward manhood and developed as individuals.

In other ages and societies, a boy became a man by participating in some sort of ancient ritual: You prepared for your first hunt, or received a tattoo, or read from the Talmud. In many cases, all of the older men in the tribe—grandfathers and uncles as well as fathers—took an active part in passing something along to you. Today not only do we lack formal rites of passage, but our fathers often fail to pass on anything at all besides a feeling of emptiness—a legacy of longing and anger and loss, of unfulfilled expectation for something we didn't even know how to ask for and which they didn't know how to give.

Today, being a man can mean something very different: It often calls for strength, but also requires being strong enough to express occasional weakness or doubt. It encompasses a broader base of experiences, including sensitivity and emotion. Having discovered how much richer manhood can be and having seen beyond the narrow view adopted by previous generations, many of the men I've grown up with hunger for what we missed. Finding nothing to emulate, we may instead rebel against who our fathers are, and become individuals in that way.

Knowing, suddenly, what is possible between people, many of us wish we'd had a different kind of relationship with our fathers. If we're honest enough to admit we still crave this, and lucky enough still to have the opportunity, many of us seek to change that relationship based on what we've learned, on who we've become. We want our fathers now to be—and to *have been*—different. But when they simply behave as they always have, in the only way they know how to behave, we become disappointed and frustrated anew. Finally recognizing what's possible between fathers and sons, we resent our dads for living and relating to us according to worn old patterns. We grow angry that they're not capable of (or maybe don't desire) the broader and richer lives we want for ourselves.

In fact, without even recognizing it as such, many men seek to change their relationships with their fathers much earlier. Ever since my dad really taught me to play golf at age twelve, a couple of years after my startling sand shot in Miami Beach, I've competed against him relentlessly. But for many years, no matter how much my own game progressed, I always lost to my father. He'd play ten strokes better than his handicap against me, and I'd always slice a couple of drives OB trying to impress him with my distance and so score ten strokes higher than usual. His psychological edge seemed unassailable. Our contests were largely unspoken, and there was never any animosity, but one measure of our relationship was that I wanted to break through the barrier that prevented me from beating him. I wanted to pass him by on my way to some great accomplishment; that is what growing up means to a young man. Perhaps, too, I sought to change our relationship so as to become my father's friend, his equal, by besting him at the game he first taught me to play.

Some things about this particular trip to Minnesota hint at such changes. We're visiting Grand View Lodge, for example, because I'm on assignment for one of the golf magazines I write for, and I've invited my father along as my guest. We're playing on my turf, so to speak; my life has arranged this outing, and I'm the one signing for the room. I know it must please my father, who has been mildly obsessed with golf for his entire life, that not only have I embraced the game but I also earn a good part of my living from it. I think he is amazed every time he sees my byline on magazine stories about golf courses in places as far-flung as Nepal and Oregon, Arizona and Côte d'Ivoire. The very love of the game that took me to all those places, and to this one, is a gift from him—one of the very few things we really share, that he managed to offer and I managed to accept.

Before it occurred to me to invite my dad along on this particular trip, I'd been thinking about a man nicknamed Gumby, whom I met while researching a magazine story on handicapped scuba divers down in the Caribbean a few years back. When he was in high school, Gumby had been a scratch golfer, with aspirations to take a shot at the tour. He'd just received a golf scholarship to college, and was beginning to envision his life around the game he loved so much. When I met him some twenty-five years later, you could still detect a certain lanky confidence—that kind of cocky good humor common to tour players—in the way Gumby moved in his wheelchair.

The world had changed for him in every way when, at age eighteen, he had been left paraplegic by a car accident. The accident took away, among many other more important things, his ability to play golf.

As we sat at a bar looking out over the turquoise waters off Bonaire, Gumby told me that what he missed most was not the lost opportunity to become a player, not the dreamed-of future, not the possibility of competition, big money, or an applauding gallery; it was the simple act of golfing with his dad. They had never been close, Gumby said, and golf had been the one thing they shared. Since his accident, since they stopped playing together, he and his father hadn't managed to get along very well anymore.

Like so many fathers and sons, my dad and I couldn't be much more different from each other. He went into his father's business; stayed in the New York area, where he was raised; married; had two children whose Little League games he always attended (though the coaches barely ever played me); put my brother and me through college; and paid off the thirty-year mortgage on his first and only home.

I am still single at age thirty-four; have never held a real job in my life; move from city to city with apparent casualness; and run away to other places whenever I get the chance.

My dad is traditional, conservative, dependable; I question everything and make few commitments. We have virtually nothing in common except golf, and our differences are obvious even in the way we approach the game.

For my father, golf is something to distract him for a few hours each Sunday, a way to get outside with his friends in the fresh salt air that blows off the wetlands surrounding his club on Long Island. He plays the same golf course week after week after week—another measure of his steady, solid character. Several times each season, he'll glean a tip from one of the golf magazines I write for, saying that he got his new chipping style from Chi Chi—as if they were old pals.

My game is wildly erratic. I'll play four holes in a row at one under par and then rack up a pair of quadruple bogeys because it takes me three shots to get off the tee or out of the sand. For me, the game itself isn't nearly as important as where it takes me—both physically and philosophically. I love the transcendent potential, which is something my father probably wouldn't consciously understand. I love the way you can play golf in the most remote surroundings, yet it's still the same game it would be on the bright, manicured fairways of the nicest country club. I love the levels beyond the fairway that my dad would probably admit had never occurred to him.

My dad, in essence, *is* the fairway. I am like the wild grass that begins at its edges and moves off into deeper rough.

Still, the game has room for many visions, and I used to imagine that playing together would provide an opportunity for my dad and me to get to know each other, and that it might somehow provide the catalyst for the change in our relationship that I've always hoped for. I imagined that, driving between holes in a golf cart, he would impart some kind of wisdom to me, that we'd express our tightly guarded emotions and nobody but the game would know.

Nothing quite so obvious has happened—which isn't to say that nothing's happened at all.

In recent years, as I've begun playing a little more seriously and my dad has slowed down from his arthritis and a couple of rounds of minor surgery, the balance of power has finally shifted. As much as he still struggles to improve, my father is losing his grip on the game. When we play together a few times a year now, I usually beat him by eight or ten strokes.

My dad still loves golf as much as anyone I've ever met, and it saddens me to realize that he will probably never get much better at it than he is now, at age seventy, and that maybe he'll never be as good as he's dreamed was possible over nearly four decades of play. Of course, he never mentions any of this, but I'm learning to intuit some of the things I wish he'd talk about.

He is proud when I beat him—if I've played well—and makes a kind of ceremony out of paying me the two or three dollars I've won. He may brag about my long drives to the other men in his Sunday foursome. At dinner, he'll tell my mother about one or another of the shots I hit, and she'll smile indulgently, perhaps marveling at this strange thing between men.

An early step in evolving as a man simply involves realizing how rich a relationship can be, and being brave enough to want that richness. Many men accomplish this when they fall in love, are grateful for what they've found, and don't choose to look back. Others of us are determined and naive and maybe stupid enough still to want more from our fathers now that *we're* capable of something more.

At the same time, some men also recognize that what's excitingly possible in our own lives may not be so for our fathers, and at this point an entirely deeper level of evolution can occur. By accepting our fathers with all their limitations, and what they want and are capable of, we can cause anger and disappointment and regret to fall away so that for the first time we see our dads differently—truly, beyond subjectivism, for the men they really are. And in so doing—in moving beyond rebellion and seeing beyond subjectivism to the simple, realistic, and transcendent Zenness of the relationship—we more fully become our individualistic selves.

Ultimately, the responsibility for changing our relationships with our fathers lies purely within ourselves. Many of us—regardless of our efforts—will never have the fathers we want; possibly no man ever really does. So we can spend our lives in anger and resentment even if our dads are guilty of nothing more than being themselves. We can also fail to see how, in their own subtle and possibly limited ways, our fathers express love differently than we might want them to, but manage to express it all the same. We can also fail to offer it back to them in a way they'll understand.

When our fathers talk to us about power tools and mutual funds, real estate and fishing, carpentry and golf, we can choose to see this as evidence of their failure to relate to us directly on an emotional level, but we can also choose to see it as their way of expressing a love they might not have the capacity to share in any other way or to talk about. In many families, these are the rituals that connect sons with their fathers, and dads with their sons—men who without such rituals, such koans of fatherhood, would have even less in common.

As we ride in the golf cart in silence from the tee box up to the seventh green at Grand View Lodge, I think about my father's round so far today. He's collected a small pile of double bogeys already. He topped a fairway iron on the third hole, knocked his drive on number four into the woods, and flubbed a pitch shot just off the sixth green (Chi Chi's fault, I said to myself). Of course, he's hit some good ones, too, and I wonder if there is any greater pleasure in the world than what my dad feels when he punches out an admirable drive or chips in from thirty yards away—especially if he needed the shot to win the hole. In fact, those are some of the few times when he can't control and suppress his emotions and I really know what he feels.

We walk onto the putting surface, where both our white golf balls stand out against the fluorescent color of the green. Sometimes it is a perfect world and there's simply nothing to say, nothing else, even, to want.

I'm actually nervous when my father steps up to stalk the line of his putt. For a moment, as he stands over his shiny X-out, I see him clearly, without the aura of illusion that sons so often reserve for their dads. I see him as a gentle, generous, loving father, a man who has never really let himself feel very much, who passionately wants to do things the right way, the good way, who wants to be closer to people, and to me, but just doesn't know how.

Someday my dad will not be out here with me. Someday I won't even be able to call him from a scrubby, unknown golf course out in the strange universe—as I've done from Texas and Idaho and Thailand—to tell him I just sunk my first eagle, or broke my own personal best, and to hear his pride in me. But even then, even when I'm alone in the world in a way that all men must eventually be alone in the world—without a father—he'll know when I've played well, because my dad will always be someplace inside of my swing.

On the fairway, we play that very traditional Scottish game called golf. Simultaneously, beyond that fairway, we share something unspoken—a love for this game that in all its mythical beauty helps us to communicate a love for each other.

When he finally sets his stance and strokes the ball, I will it to break and fall into the cup the same way he must have willed me toward a smooth, natural swing at the driving range twenty years ago. It surprises me to realize that I am rooting for my father to play his very best.

I'm hoping that he makes ten birdies. I'm hoping that he kicks my butt.

CHAPTER TEN

Not-Golfing

In Zen, there are no borders between "teacher" and "student"; we are all working together to learn for ourselves.

—*K. T. Berger*, Zen Driving

One day assistant pro Osho went for a walk in the rugged terrain just beyond the golf course. On his return to the pro shop, the Head Pro said to him: "Osho, where have you been?"

"I've been walking out beyond the golf course," Osho replied.

"Where did you go?" the Head Pro inquired curiously.

"Going, I followed the fragrant grasses; returning, I pursued the falling blossoms," answered Osho.

"How very springlike the feeling," exclaimed the Head Pro.

"Still better is the dripping of autumn dew

from the full-blown lotus flowers,'' returned
Osho.

"I am grateful to you for your answer," the
Head Pro said.

—*Zen golf koan*

DRIVING NORTH ON UTAH HIGHWAY 191, THE ROAD SLICES
through a rugged, barren landscape of redrock buttes,
steep talus slopes, sagebrush, and cacti. The sun is merciless,
and the creek beds are all dry.

My friend Leon and I have just emerged from eight days of
wilderness backpacking in the kilnlike desert heat—up and
down steep, remote canyons with forty-pound loads strapped
to us, searching for ancient Native American ruins, cutting
ourselves on prickly pear and sharp rocks. We have not shaved
or showered in over a week. We have not changed clothes.
We've eaten only freeze-dried food and drunk only muddy
stream water treated with iodine to kill harmful bacteria.

But now that we've returned to the world (or gone out of
it, as Leon would contend) we are driving fast in a battered
pickup truck toward the town of Moab, not to pamper ourselves, not questing after cheeseburgers or milk shakes or cold
beers, not to bathe or call our families or sleep in beds, but
for the sole purpose of trying to squeeze in eighteen holes of
golf before dark. Golf has become a meditative practice for
us, and our transition back to civilization after emerging from
the wilderness.

Dust seems to fly from our hair in the breeze blowing in
through the windows. As we speed through the desolate countryside Leon turns to me and asks earnestly, "Does this seem
completely normal?"

159

And I know he is talking about the fact that we play golf.

A club member taking lessons with the Head Pro asked, "What does one think of while golfing?"

"One thinks of not-golfing," the Head Pro replied.

"How does one think of not-golfing?" the member asked.

"Without thinking, without golfing," the Head Pro said.

—*Zen golf koan*

Leon is many things to many different people: river guide, ex-boyfriend, radical environmentalist, Outward Bound instructor, professional photographer, dependable friend. He is, in fact, many different things even to me, but no manifestation is more important than his role as the not-golfer, in which he is dedicated to opposing every religiously held tenet of the Royal and Ancient Game. Partly caught up in maya and subjectivism, Leon hates the very idea of golf and all that he imagines it represents—corporate America, environmental indifference, red meat, Republicans, Barry Manilow, Mormons, lawyers, the Glen Canyon Dam, and plaid polyester pants. At the same time, though, a sad accident of fate (or perhaps it's no accident?) has also left him helplessly addicted to the game. Golf is a secret obsession of which he is ashamed. If we ever meet up with his friends after golfing, he will lie about where we've been. Is this Crazy Cloud Zen? Or just crazy? If they ever invent a support group for golfers, he will be the first to stand up at their meetings and admit, "My name is Leon, and I am an eighteen handicap" (although he's more like a twenty-four).

In his paradoxical and self-appointed role as not-golfer, Leon will instinctively display revulsion any time I mention the possibility of our playing golf. In person, he'll scrunch up his face as if he's just swallowed something that flew into his mouth; over the telephone, he'll emit a high-pitched sort of whining sound meant to communicate his disdain. But in spite of his attitude, Leon—not fully enlightened yet—still occasionally gives in to practical, subsidiary aims, and plays.

Because he stands at the opposite extreme of the realms inhabited by most people who ever pick up a set of clubs, Leon plays golf out in unmanicured terrain, where it is a very different game—though not any easier for a lefty who swings too fast. To me (and he will surely hate this) Leon is a beacon, a blinking beam of illumination reminding me, at moments when I'm self-absorbed enough to think of *myself* as someone who plays beyond the fairway, of how incredibly much further into unmanicured terrain I can still penetrate. Leon will also hate the idea that he is a living tribute to the flexibility of the game, a perfect, shining example that golf is not what it might appear to be when viewed through normal perceptions. Still, he is a recalcitrant teacher, though I know well the very point he won't fess up (a point I sometimes wonder if he even consciously recognizes himself): that his not-golfing has a higher philosophical purpose. That it's a statement about the transcendent nature of reality, a road sign pointing the way toward enlightenment. If I were to ask him where the true path lies, he might very well respond, "Not-golfing." The problem is that he lacks the iron discipline to maintain permanently the difficult and elusive pure not-golfing state.

The fact that Leon plays at all—however resignedly, however awkwardly—is the best supporting evidence for the thesis I'm trying to expound upon in this book. If you don't believe or understand what I've been saying, I challenge you to invite him for eighteen holes at your country club; the experience is guaranteed to forever alter your vision of the game. Because Leon, himself, *is* a golf koan.

The couple of times each year that he and I actually play together, he likes to believe that we never really intended to, but somehow circumstances conspired to force us into it. He blames the golf on me, and I'm glad I can be of some use to him. Our games always occur just after we've finished a backcountry adventure, usually some highly impractical and potentially dangerous trip in the wilderness. We take great pride in playing, whenever possible, on the worst courses in America, in towns most people have never heard of, as if these layouts were remote and austere hermitages designed for pursuing this particular form of moving meditation, for exploring the paradox of golfing/not-golfing, and for focusing on the direct experience of nature, which provides the backdrop to our golf journeys and further inspires us both.

> In the spring beyond time,
> The withered tree flowers.
> —*Zen Saying*

Moab Golf Club, in Moab, Utah, is among the courses we love best, as much for its own immense beauty as for the surrounding wilderness. The holes, alternately friendly and menacing, climb high up along sandstone mesas, drop into gullies, and curl around blue lakes. Each fairway carves a spongy emerald oasis into the harsh topography, and the greens are ringed with traps the deep red color of the surrounding rock. Missing these fairways is more than inconvenient; something tries to bite, scrape, stab, or puncture us every time we venture into the rough, where golf and wilderness truly meet. So we move slowly, making enough noise to warn the rattlesnakes of our approach.

For Leon and me, there's another highlight to the Moab course: a lake about 250 yards from the eighth tee contains some of the largest bullfrogs we have ever seen—frogs as big as Thanksgiving turkeys, with voices like the bugles of approaching cavalry.

Most golfers would not consider such factors in recommending a course.

But we are not most golfers.

Echoing across the canyons, cactus flowers bloom.

At the limits of heaven the sun rises and the moon sets. Beyond the balustrade the mountains deepen and the waters become chill.

—Zen saying

Many of our golf destinations aren't what you'd call upscale. This is fine (even requisite) with Leon, who plays in gym shorts, a gauze-thin Greenpeace T-shirt, and the same Teva sandals he wears while hiking, rafting, and eating in restaurants. In general, Leon is not big on making concessions; he'd guffaw at the notion of making any to the fashion etiquette or expense of golf—a sport he is truly and deeply sorry that he loves. Sometimes I catch him hitting over water hazards with range balls that have inexplicably wandered into his bag.

BEYOND THE FAIRWAY

We play at the Lajitas Golf Course in Lajitas, Texas, throughout one particular spring, on days when we are not guiding raft trips on the Rio Grande River for Big Bend River Tours, a company that Leon owned for about three weeks until he realized the implications. Grass grows only sporadically on this scrubby nine-hole course, and the greens play nearly as slow as the sand bunkers—which they resemble, except that they're not as well-manicured. But every hole offers a view of the Mesa de Anguilla, through which the Rio Grande carves one of the narrowest and most spectacular gorges on this planet.

Beneath the night sky, the river runs deepest.

Endlessly rise the distant mountains,
Blue heaped upon blue.
                                    —Zen saying

I have never seen Leon opt for a penalty stroke when any other choice is available—as if each challenge of hitting from behind a tree or up against a boundary fence might reveal something to him. At Alpine Meadows Golf Course in Enterprise, Oregon, I watch as he plays a shot from the bottom of a ravine, underneath a wooden footbridge, with no physical possibility of escape. To Leon, taking a penalty stroke would represent an unpardonable breach of honor, like one of the marathon monks of Mount Hiei failing to complete his run. Leon would sooner throw trash on the ground or wear a Lacoste shirt. I think he sees penalty strokes as a metaphor of some sort involving questions of philosophy and religious faith. When he hits a three wood out of the ravine—I swear this is true—his golf ball ex-

164

plodes, and we're left with the task of interpreting what this means. Leon thinks it's simply hilarious. I see the implications of complete transcendence and experience a brief moment of enlightenment.

We play Alpine Meadows after hiking around the awesome Wallowa Mountains, which surround the course with blue peaks still capped by snow in June. The lush fairways, where cows would certainly graze if they could pay the greens fees, cross musical Trout Creek several times. Marmots cavort in the cold water, perhaps searching for golf balls to sell.

The snow melts in the mountains, making the stream waters sing.

> Ten years searching
>   in the deep forest
> Today great laughter at
>   the edge of the lake.
> —*Soen*

We never exactly *plan* to play golf. We each just happen to bring our clubs. We stow them under backpacks and rafting gear, tents and sleeping bags, Ziploc bags full of rice and instant potatoes. And then we raft or hike or rock climb, but in the back of our minds we think about golf. We dream of the smooth roll of the ball along soft grass, the clean feel of a well-arced chip shot. In the silence of rivers and mountains, forests and lakes and canyons, we can practically hear the sound of a twenty-foot putt dropping into the cup: only slightly louder than the sound of one hand clapping.

From some of the raised tees at the Bryden Canyon Golf Course, in Lewiston, Idaho, we spot a calm stretch of the

Snake River glinting below in the high-desert light. Several hundred miles upstream from here the river disappears into Hell's Canyon, where we just finished guiding a six-day rafting trip for Northwest Dories, one of America's premier river outfitters. Above Wild Sheep Rapid—a mess of whitewater frothing with liquid muscle—Leon pointed out the least dangerous route. He is a far more experienced boatman, so I deferred to his advice. But on the fourth hole at Bryden Canyon, drawing on something I learned at the Innisbrook Golf Institute, I instruct Leon that if he opens his stance just a bit, he might correct a tendency toward slicing. We are both students, both teachers. On this day, Leon loses a ball in the rough beyond one of the fairways, and might search for it indefinitely if I don't offer him a free drop.

The most memorable hole on the course features a sharp dogleg that turns and drops so precipitously we can't see the fairway or the flag. The greenskeeper has erected a round metal sign, painted with a bull's-eye, to help us aim. I can't help wondering if bells ring and we win a free round for actually hitting the bull's-eye. At Bryden Canyon we also love the jackrabbits that live in the sagebrush; they march down the fairway in front of us like Arnie's Army, only with longer ears.

Beneath the August sun, silver rabbit hair glints as if in moonlight.

On another occasion, Fuke, who came and went as he pleased, sometimes joining Rinzai's assembly, but mostly hanging around the marketplace, was sitting outside the meditation hall chomping on raw cabbage. Rinzai saw him and called out, "You have quite the air of an ass!"

Fuke started to bray. Rinzai shouted, "This robber!"
And Fuke took off, calling loudly, "Robber, robber!"

No mere exercise in one-upmanship, this kind of encounter served as a fine opportunity for sharpening Zen
insight.

—*Perle Besserman and Manfred Steger,*
Crazy Clouds: Zen Radicals, Rebels, and Reformers

The murmuring of the spring as the night deepens,
The coloring of the hills as the sun goes down.
—*Zen saying*

Our golf ritual includes a prolonged period of haggling over
how many strokes I should give Leon, and what we should
bet. When we play the par-three Civiton Golf Course in Farmington, New Mexico, we've just come off a week of very
rugged backpacking on the Navajo Indian Reservation. Instead
of wagering money or dinner, we agree to this: If Leon wins,
we will camp in the evening along the side of some dirt road
outside of town. If I win, we'll share a motel room, which
I'll probably end up paying for anyway.

I don't have my clubs in Farmington, so I search for a rental
set in which at least two of the clubs were made by the same
manufacturer. No luck. Leon happily reminds me that he's
playing with the same short clubs he used as a kid—clubs that
he sold once because he didn't like the idea of owning them,
but repurchased several years later, turning a small profit.

We play Farmington's nine holes twice, long into the warm
evening, toward that moment when the sunset nostalgically re-
calls every lovely place we've ever been. Plates clatter in the
kitchens of houses nearby, and the air is like a gin and tonic.

The most exciting aspect of this course is the way the tee boxes have been placed so close to the greens. Each time we tee off, we must simultaneously scout for incoming balls. There is a certain challenge to this; it adds an aspect of defense, which golf usually lacks. I am not allowed to say who won our bet, but I've always found—and this evening is no different—that Super 8 Motels offer comfortable rooms at very reasonable rates.

With first darkness, even the crickets hush.

At every step the pure wind rises.
                                        —*Zen saying*

For years now, Leon has described a course he passed once in Mt. Carmel Junction, Utah, just north of the Arizona border. After consulting topographical maps, he's figured out that a week-long backpack trip through Parunuweap Canyon could bring us out of the wilderness practically in the parking lot next to the clubhouse. He talks about this adventure the way honeymooners describe upcoming trips to Fiji or Bora-Bora.

Leon is currently devising a way to carry a full set of clubs comfortably on a backpack for seven days. He's even suggested that we actually *golf* our way through the entire length of Parunuweap. So we're negotiating how many strokes I should give him over the twenty-three miles of rocky, highly unmanicured terrain.

But I wonder: How many strokes will he need if we traverse the canyon not-golfing?

CHAPTER ELEVEN

Far East Meets Wild West

Chop wood,
Carry water.

—Zen saying

At a golf club where there were two separate
courses, two golfers—one playing the East
Course and one playing the West Course—met in
a patch of rough common to both layouts. They
began arguing over a golf ball.

The Head Pro came along, heard them arguing,
and said, "If you can speak, I'll spare the golf
ball. If not, I'll knock it into the lake."

Neither golfer replied, so the Head Pro hit a
towering wedge shot into the middle of the
water.

That evening, assistant pro Zhaozhou came
back from giving lessons, and the Head Pro told
him what had happened. Zhaozhou then took off
his golf shoes, put them on his head, and walked
out.

BEYOND THE FAIRWAY

The Head Pro said, "Had you been there, you
could have saved the golf ball."

—*Zen golf koan*

IN A BOOK ENTITLED *ECOTOPIA*, ERNEST CALLENBACH TELLS THE
story of a futuristic Pacific Northwest that secedes from the
United States. Callenbach reasons that the upper left corner
of our nation could achieve self-sufficiency while supporting a
lifestyle far better than what's possible in the rest of the country.

For one thing, the Northwest is blessed with an embarrassing richness of natural resources and products—cedar and
Douglas fir, Chinook salmon and Dungeness crab, Walla Walla
sweet onions (the best in the world), and many excellent pinot
noirs. For another thing, residents of this vast, remote, and
powerfully beautiful region express the kind of rugged individualism that's become scarce in America since the closing of
the frontier a century ago.

In fact, the historian Frederick Jackson Turner believed that
Americans developed a particularly individualistic character in
response to the wild lands and open spaces that were so plen-
tiful beyond the Mississippi River, the Rocky Mountains, and
the hundredth meridian. In the 1990s, while much of our
nation has come to derive its character from malls and con-
venience stores, residents of the Pacific Northwest remain
closely connected to the land—the region's very soul and the
source of its own damp and quirky individualism. The Northwest remains largely unmanicured; it is beyond the neat,
sprawling fairways enveloping so much of America. And the
spirit of western individualism lives on in the Northwest not
only through men such as my friend Leon and Jack Stallings,

not only through loggers, fishermen, river guides, and other true individualists, but also through the land itself. The region's particularly rugged individualism is largely born of place.

It's as easy to overlook how intrinsic this independent, maverick nature is to local inhabitants as it is to misjudge how deeply rooted northwesterners are in the land. In reporting on the timber controversy currently raging throughout the Northwest, for example, the national media have missed an essential point: that the controversy is not about environmental regulations, spotted owls, or even the timber economy so much as it's about the spirit of northwesterners. It's about the threat to an unconstrained way of life in which a man can work in the woods and earn his living from his own labor on the land—even though logging, through irresponsible management, has become outmoded and harmful to the very ecology so important to inhabitants.

Certain inherent incompatibilities would seem to exist between Eastern philosophy and western individualism. Among other differences, the hierarchical structure of Zen, its focus on meditation and retreat rather than on action and confrontation, its concepts of transcendence and the notion of a single all-inclusive Reality, and its antiquated attitudes toward women (to name a few) would seem to put it in direct conflict with such American ideals as independence, democracy, civil disobedience, and other expressions of the individual—some of which may involve a certain amount of ego attachment. These differences should prove even more divisive in the American West, which is a symbol and a wellspring of individualism. However, the Zen notion that we should each pursue our own personal paths and serve as our own authorities provides a

171

chance to reconcile such apparent mutual exclusions. In terms of the journey toward enlightenment, Zen encourages individualism, and individualism reflects at least an aspect of Zen. To take this one step further, if the land in the Northwest is a source of such individualism, it should also reveal aspects of Zen. Finally, some of the individualistic I-N-G adventure sports—such as golfing and skiing—seem to provide a common ground where aspects of East and West can meet in kinship.

All of which may seem a little beside the point to golfers in the Northwest, who display a renegade, nonconformist attitude, likely born of their wild, free lands. For instance, unlike in most places where it may actually rain for more than seven days in a single week, when golfers in the upper left corner see storm clouds threatening, they simply pull on their Gore-Tex before heading out to the course. Weather forecasters in Oregon actually differentiate between "rain" and "showers"; to local golfers, showers—which are heavier—mean hitting an extra club.

Taking a closer look at one western golf individualist and at some of the golf venues that may have given rise to this particular kind of player may provide some insight into the koan of Northwestern golfing and the way East and West can complement each other.

> The way of Zen may be the most effective avenue to driving, but then driving itself is the best way to learn Zen. . . . Ultimately, your contented driving experience can spill over into other areas of your life. . . . Zen driving is a form of meditation/yoga everyone can do. . . . In short, and it may sound a bit corny or farfetched, you can improve the quality of

your life through proper driving practice. Better living
through better driving.

—K. T. Berger, Zen Driving

Ever since he was a boy, Zen golf philosopher and single-
digit handicapper Jim Waldron, from Enterprise, Oregon, has
dreamed of owning his own driving range. Surely some northwesterners cherish grander visions, but his typifies the individualistic, lifestyle-oriented goals held by many Ecotopians. And
Waldron's golf individualism—like all western individualism—is clearly based in the land, which in this case has caused
a few problems.

In the book *Zen Driving,* K. T. Berger writes about driving
a car, but the fact that his words often apply just as aptly to
driving a golf ball provides a neat bit of synchronicity. Taking
this a step further, the term *driving range* can assume several
deeper meanings when considered closely. It might, for example, refer to the range or scope of someone's driving. The
word *driving* itself might refer to driving a car or a golf ball
or, at a deeper level, to the kind of drive that compels people
to pursue a particular dream. Thus, *driving range* may also
indicate exactly how far a person can go.

Waldron's driving range dream is complicated by the fact that
Wallowa County, Oregon, supports a population of only around
7,000, and only a few hundred of them play golf. Still, Waldron
believes the evidence points toward golf in the county really taking off. Whereas he used to head out to the Alpine Meadows
Golf Course in Enterprise (a venue where I golfed with my
friend Leon) at six in the evening and play four or five balls at a
time on each hole, traffic on the links has increased to the point
where this is now only occasionally feasible.

173

In wanting to own a driving range, Jim Waldron seems to have several different things in mind. He imagines his range as the neighborhood watering hole of driving ranges—a place where folks could come to practice their golf swings, take lessons, and exchange ideas about the game, a sort of monastery ground where individuals pursuing their own golf lives might come to meet and "do the community thing," as Waldron puts it. In the wild American West of the nineteenth century, even the individualistic mountain men rendezvoused occasionally to swap stories, trade pelts, and perhaps discuss their short games.

About two years ago, Waldron began looking to lease land on which to build his driving range, but soon discovered that "it was like trying to buy property on the moon." Ranchers who owned most of the parcels near the golf course found it hard to believe that anyone would actually pay to hit golf balls. And for another thing, they couldn't understand why anyone in his right mind would agree to pay two or three times the going rate for leasing land, as Waldron offered to do, just to compensate for the extra tax that the landowner would have to pay for taking good agricultural plots out of production.

Confronted with these early hurdles, Waldron scrambled to find a piece of land farther away. Realizing that a range located at any distance from the golf course wouldn't be as economically viable, he decided to create his own golf school, which he could market to tourists in combination with outdoor adventure trips into the nearby Wallowa Mountains and on the Snake River.

He finally found an appropriate piece of property in neighboring Joseph, and the owner seemed amenable to Waldron's impassioned explanation of his dream—so much so, in fact, that a few weeks later the man submitted his own use permit application for a driving range to the local planning commission, although he didn't know the first thing about golf. He proposed a ten-station range only eighty yards wide, which might have worked fine if nobody in the county ever had a tendency to hook or slice.

In case this whole matter wasn't already complicated enough, while Waldron was busy fighting the other land use application, one of the two realtors he'd hired found another potential site. Unfortunately, the land was so good that the local soil commission had awarded it the highest possible rating for agricultural use, and Waldron's life partner, Jean, an environmental activist, was committed to a local grass-roots effort opposing the development of such prime agricultural land. At the same time, the landowner was afraid to take the plot out of agricultural production because he didn't know whether he'd be able to reclaim his tax deferral if the driving range failed, or even after the ten-year lease with Waldron expired.

The tenacious Waldron devised an ingenious solution: He proposed keeping his driving range open on this land from eight A.M. to eight P.M. Upon closing, he'd then herd a flock of sheep onto the property and leave them to graze until he came back to chase them out in the morning, before reopening the driving range. The sheep would not only maintain the grass—thereby eliminating the need for mowing—but would also constitute an agricultural use of the land, satisfying both Jean and the landowner. However, this deal ultimately fell through.

Meanwhile, against Waldron's advice to the contrary, the planning commission approved the other driving range. But by then he was nearly ready to close another lease arrangement—until a notoriously sleazy lawyer killed it at the last moment because he and Waldron had once tussled over a real-estate deal and Waldron had recommended that the lawyer give up his practice and pursue a career as a Jerry Lewis impersonator.

According to Waldron, the driving range in Joseph hasn't done very well since opening, and will probably fold pretty soon: It's overpriced and too far from the golf course, and many local golfers won't frequent it because the owner stole Waldron's idea. But recently a landowner with a parcel adjacent to the golf course began suggesting that he might open a range after all. In return for free practice balls for life and the opportunity to teach lessons there, Waldron is willing to get the new range up and running.

Meanwhile, as he waits this out, Waldron traded one lonely, individualistic dream for another: He's currently writing a book about Zen golf.

Crazy Cloud Zen illustrates that meditation is a living experience, neither limited to monasteries and temples, nor bounded by time and national borders.

—*Perle Besserman and Manfred Steger,*
Crazy Clouds: Zen Radicals, Rebels, and Reformers

If, as Ernest Callenbach has imagined, Oregon and Washington ever establish their own sovereignty, the region's individualistic golfers also can achieve self-sufficiency, because the upper left corner contains nearly every type of golf course imaginable: windswept links layouts; tracts carved out of the big timber of the northern rain forests; lush, flat valley courses with plenty of water; venues stretched across the dusty buttes of the high desert; and alpine courses undulating beneath snowy mountain peaks. Many of these golf courses are as quirky and unique as the local populace, and equally as dependent on the topography for their personalities. They could serve as perfect temples for pursuing Zen golf, since each strange location is like a golf koan in itself.

Outside of Salem, Oregon, for example, one country club actually buries members along its fairways. The Oregon golf menu also includes odd courses such as Devil's Lake, a thirteen-hole layout, and Bayou Golf Club, haunted by its very own ghost. In Washington, engineers constructed the Three Rivers Golf Course on ash and debris from Mt. St. Helens (the volcano is no longer considered a hazard). McCormick Woods, near Seattle, boasts its own naturalist on staff. And the Inn at Semiahmoo, a five-star resort just south of the Canadian border, was formerly a salmon cannery.

Salishan Lodge, along the Oregon coast, is unique because it may be the only five-star *motel* in America. I visited Salishan with Leon, who was serving as the photographer for a magazine story I was writing. Leon had never stayed anyplace nicer than hostelries with numbers in their names. He was genuinely impressed—so much so that in our room he cleaned up the crumbs from a week-old French bread he'd pulled out of his truck for lunch, and made yet another exception to not-golfing.

During our visit, the requisite Pacific storm settled over the coast. Fog clung to the nearby mountains, a salty gray sky pressed down on us, and rain fell musically through cedar, pine, and spruce, which, in Oregon, isn't an acceptable reason not to play golf.

Salishan's layout actually consists of two very different nines. The front weaves through a hilly evergreen forest and feels quintessentially northwestern; loggers would grow nostalgic amid this scenery. The back nine emulates a Scottish links course and features thick roughs, beach grass, abundant dunes and bunkers, and gusty winds. The course is sandwiched between the Pacific Ocean and Siletz Bay, and the resort is built from local wood, so it blends in with and reflects the natural character of the land.

In spite of the fact that water ran down our faces in rivulets as if we were statues in a fountain, Leon and I were not the only players out on the course—though possibly we were the coldest. What matters in Oregon is not how you play, but that you play at all. Passing fully soaked through the main lobby after our round, I waved to the desk clerk, proud that—just like locals—we'd finished eighteen holes in what seemed like a monsoon.

"Has it started raining?" he asked, barely looking up.

Most folks who've never visited Ecotopia are surprised to learn that a large part of Oregon actually consists of desert. On the east side of the Cascade mountain range—which acts as a rain fence, trapping most moisture on the fertile west side—a land of rock and scrub and sagebrush rolls much of the way to Idaho.

For a truly strange northwestern desert golf experience that expresses its own brand of rugged individualism, visit Kahneeta Lodge, the only golf resort in the world owned and operated by Native Americans (whose religious beliefs share much in common with Eastern philosophies). If Clint Eastwood had been a golfer instead of a gunfighter, he might have filmed his movies there.

Although neither the golf course nor the resort bring the word *posh* to mind, the distinctly unbridled western flavor refreshes like a cold stream. The golf course itself is flat, open, and dry, but at least golf balls travel farther, making players feel young and powerful. Many holes meander along the Warm Springs River, and while Leon (once again dressed up as my photographer) and I were playing one such par four, a group of resort guests floated by in kayaks. We felt silly to be caught playing golf, and wished we were kayaking, too. Kahneeta also features a natural hot springs where you can pretend you've come to soak after riding across the desert for ten days on your tired but devoted horse.

Although Leon and I didn't meet up with any actual Native Americans, we did encounter a couple of pretty wild young hairdressers who were drinking tequila shots in the bar. I interpreted this as a sign that they were out to have some unrestrained fun in Kahneeta's freewheeling western locale. As always, the landscape exerted its influence, and the four of us ended up drinking homemade liquor on the balcony off of our room and watching a humongous yellow moon rise up over distant buttes. In the expansive, lawless topography of the undeveloped West, anything can happen. And it did.

Once when the wind was whipping the flag on the eighteenth green, the Head Pro witnessed two assistant pros debating about it. One said the flag was moving, one said the wind was moving.

They argued back and forth without attaining the principle, so the Head Pro said, "This is not the movement of the wind, nor the movement of the flag; it is the movement of your minds.''

The two assistant pros were awestruck.

—*Zen golf koan*

More than any other golf course among the varied, individualistic layouts of the region, Port Ludlow, on Washington's Olympic Peninsula, best expresses the rugged Pacific northwestern character. Built by lumber barons Pope and Talbot— perhaps as penance for cutting down so many trees—this hugely difficult, large-scale venue was carved out of a forest of towering cedar and fir, and planted with explosions of native wildflowers. Rated in the top 1 percent of the nation's courses by the American Society of Golf Course Architects, Ludlow overflows with unrestrained personality. Gigundo cedar and fir snags guard some greens and dogleg turns, and may make you wish you knew a lumberjack nearby. While playing there with my friend John Hayden (with whom I also visited Nepal), I witnessed the single worst lie I've ever seen. Approaching one of the difficult, half-hidden greens, we discovered John's ball actually inside a hollow cedar stump. Like any true northwesterner, John tried climbing inside this visibly manifested golf koan to see if just maybe he had a shot.

This very western outpost of golf also features its own outlaw: PGA pro Lyndon Blackwell, whose very name suggests that he should be drawing six-shooters against the sheriff in the street outside a local saloon. His weapon of choice, however, is more likely to be a six iron—and he's not afraid to use it.

On certain afternoons when the weather is warm, the sun high, and the tourists mostly on their way back to Seattle,

Blackwell and a group of admiring locals play a rather ruthless skins game into which unsuspecting city folk (John and I) can easily be lured. A sense of untempered freedom characterizes these rounds, as if you're beyond the reach of the rules of golf and the laws of Washington State. Blackwell's advice for playing Port Ludlow is to be conservative because the course "eats greedy players alive." My advice is not to underestimate Herbie, the unassuming greenskeeper, who can often be found counting his winnings in the bar.

After playing our fifth round of golf in seventy-two hours—and paying off our debts to Lyndon and Herbie—we drove away in the early evening, headed for our friend Mosey Farris's cabin on Lake Sutherland. We stopped once along the winding, hilly route to pick up a five-pound salmon (for about three dollars) and some ice-cold Henry Weinhart's Ale.

On our way south, though, John got a speeding ticket on one of the remote, curving roads that wind through (what's left of) the old-growth forests on the Olympic Peninsula. As a burly state trooper wrote up the summons, John shook his head for a few moments before mustering the courage to express what was on his mind.

"I don't know if you play golf, Officer," he said. "But I've been driving horrendously all day." (I was surprised that he didn't even mention his putting.)

Mosey had already fired up the barbecue by the time we arrived, and we drank frosty Henrys, tossed a salad, made garlic bread, and prepared some fresh corn while the salmon grilled.

After enjoying all this regional bounty from the land and waters of the Northwest, we built a fire in the sauna out on the back deck and drank a few more icy beers in the smooth cedar enclosure until the temperature grew so wonderfully and unbearably hot that we flung the door open, sprinted nakedly across the deck, and plunged into the lake. The chilly water offered up the briefest glimpse of enlightenment, a moment of experience so direct, so real, a fleeting instant in which the opposites of lake and sky, hot and cold, darkness and light, individualistic and communal, west and east, yin and yang, merged and then fell away, revealing a more durable One-ness—as if the northwestern terrain itself were offering us these insights. We were already yipping and yee-hawing when we rose to the surface beneath the glittering summer night.

CHAPTER TWELVE

The Masters

If you ask me the question, "What is kensho—
what is this 'seeing into one's own real
nature'?" I am afraid I can give you no other
answer than to say: "Kensho is just kensho,
nothing more."

—*Isshu Miura and Ruth Fuller Sasaki,*
The Zen Koan

In 1965 I was playing in the PGA Championship
at Laurel Valley just east of Pittsburgh. On the
practice tee Sam Snead was hitting balls directly
behind me. Sam said, "Roland, watch this."
With pleasure I turned around. He announced he
was going to hit a drive with a fade at the end to
slip around the dogleg on the 16th hole. He then
proceeded to hit this magnificent-looking shot
about 230 yards straight as an arrow before it
faded to the right another 30 or 40 yards.

> . . . I asked him what I thought to be a
> profound question, "How do you fade the ball?"
> He remarked smugly, "I just think fade."
> —*Roland Stafford, founder of the Roland Stafford Golf School*

A BUNCH OF MOSTLY TALL, MOSTLY STIFF, MOSTLY SHORT-haired white guys wearing a high proportion of bad slacks go out for a five-hour walk. Along the way, they stop sixty or seventy times to hit a ball with a stick.

That's one view of professional golf.

On the other hand, on the first morning of the Fred Meyer Challenge, a nontour charity event hosted by Peter Jacobsen at the Oregon Golf Club each August, John Daly was performing a long-drive exhibition on the eighteenth green. He was hitting balls from a grass platform out at—and occasionally *over*—the ladies' tee box 300 yards away. After cranking out three or four monsters, Daly teed up another ball, turned around on the platform, and announced that he was going to hit one at the radio tower rising up out of the crowd of several thousand spectators sitting along the slopes of a natural amphitheater surrounding the green.

The tower was maybe sixty feet high, one hundred yards away, and surrounded by a sea of fans. We all thought Daly was joking; even as he went into his famous backswing, folks figured that he had substituted an exploding, powder golf ball, or that he would swing so far under the ball that it would barely pop up into the air.

But folks were wrong.

Daly swung full force at a real golf ball. The crowd flinched at contact, and the shot whizzed overhead like a Scud missile, flying wide of the tower by ten feet and disappearing in the direction of the parking lot at high velocity.

Next to Daly on the stage area, Peter Jacobsen—renowned for his lightning wit and comedian's timing—stood speechless, his mouth hanging open. Jack Lemmon, on hand for the pro-am that day and also on stage with Daly, shook his head in disbelief.

"Jesus, John," he said. "You've got the guts of a burglar."

The gallery, initially stunned, eventually erupted into uncertain applause, as if they didn't quite comprehend what had just occurred.

That's the opposite extreme of what professional golf *could be*.

If a connection truly exists between golf and Eastern philosophy, then touring professionals are necessarily the most learned golf philosophers, the true Masters—in the sense of Zen Masters—of the game. As such, tour players have at least the ability, if not the responsibility, to communicate some of their vast knowledge to those of us whose understanding of golf hasn't evolved as highly. More philosophically inclined spectators at the Fred Meyer Challenge might have interpreted John Daly's stunt as just such a transmission of knowledge, as an example of Zen, albeit Crazy Zen, at work. Rather than (or in addition to) thinking Daly was stupidly showing off, a golf philosopher might have recognized that by driving a golf ball over the crowd, Daly was hurling a lightning bolt of pure communication regarding transcendence—not a lesson about it, but the clearest possible demonstration of the principle in action. As dumb as that single golf shot was, even to attempt it Daly must have transcended all subjective concerns about

185

what might have happened, and lived purely in that single moment of contact when he knew that nothing could go wrong. But such clear demonstrations of Eastern golf, those moments when the Masters offer us glimpses of their golf wisdom, in actions or in words, are rare.

Unfortunately, professional golf suffers from a serious public relations problem because it communicates an image that has little to do with the deep, true, resonant experience of playing the game. On television, in print, and in person, tournament play and most tournament players come across as bland, staid, generic, undynamic, and deadly boring to just about anyone who has even the slightest hint of a pulse. You'd never imagine that the players were enlightened in any way or that so many fans are so anxious to learn from them about the true, deep secrets of the game.

But if golf spectatorship is to grow, as it has tremendous potential to do now that so many people are taking up the sport; if professional golf hopes to compete for viewers with the kinds of high-action sports such as basketball and football that we've practically built our modern American culture around; and if amateurs are to learn anything about the true nature of the game, then the PGA Tour needs to loosen up, uncork the bubbles, pull the stick out of its butt, and explore some of the terrain beyond the safe, uncontroversial, highly manicured fairway it has staked out for itself. It needs to present pro golfers to the public as if they were real people rather than mechanical swing machines like the ones used to test golf balls. It needs to repackage golf as a spontaneous and potentially spiritual activity where anything can happen, and streamline the game's image for the 90s—and I don't mean the 1890s. It needs to assume some leadership in teaching us about the deeper levels at which golf can be played. And it needs John Daly and Peter Jacobsen and every other pro willing to exhibit even a speck of personality and individualism. Because even if you hate John Daly, chances are you don't confuse him with a hundred other players who look and act as if they've been genetically engineered.

Golf is a sport of contained fury, of controlled power. Whereas athletes in other sports can purge their frustrations and express their characters by slamming a dunk, sacking a quarterback, or kicking a soccer ball with all their pent-up energy, golfers have no outlet for the emotions that are an undeniable component of competitive play. Golf demands precision and control rather than bursts of effort and feeling. So it's understandable that golfers exhibit less personality: That is part of the internal nature of the sport.

But this tendency also distances golfers from their fans. So professional golf must discover ways for players to express their personalities, to talk about the sport more viscerally, to communicate its magic, to accept the role of revered Masters who can speak to the millions of willing students of the game. All of that would be good for golf. Achieving this may require a combined effort among the players themselves, the PGA Tour, tournament officials and sponsors, advertisers, and even the complacent cadre within the golf media—who have promoted the sleepy image of the game through their unwillingness to take chances and to pursue excellence rather than market strategies. They would rather produce one more pithy and annoying feature about the 1954 U.S. Open than take a dangerous step by experimenting with something new, with an unfamiliar, nontraditional perception.

There's no arguing the fact that John Daly's spontaneous

shot at the radio tower during the Fred Meyer Challenge was supremely boneheaded and even dangerous—not only to the spectators he might have killed with a mishit, but also to the charity tournament itself, which surely would have been a casualty had anything gone wrong. Daly is the only touring pro clueless enough to attempt such a stunt, and brazen enough to pull it off. Afterward, many people, pros and spectators alike, called Daly a loose cannon and a crazy, dumb, out-of-control kid. And you can bet that he didn't repeat that part of the exhibition the following day.

But he had no trouble finding other ways of expressing his crazy golf Zen. Three times during the pro-am, for example, he teed off over the heads of the group out on the fairway in front of him. At the charity auction held at a corporate dinner on the second night of the tournament, Daly was offering a beautiful golf print signed by several different pros. Bidding, he announced, would begin at $5,000. When nobody even opened, Daly incited the gathered corporate mucky-mucks by promising to throw in a set of his own golf clubs. And a travel bag. And twelve dozen golf balls. And two dozen gloves. When someone finally bid $6,000, Daly bid $10,000 himself to drive the price higher and shame the rich folks into shelling out. He eventually elicited $11,000 for the tournament's charities. But the next morning, this same John Daly who was so generous and energetic, who'd stopped so often during the pro-am to sign autographs or give his hat to some kid, told the crowd it was the first time he'd ever awakened sober in Portland, and he felt like shit.

Put simply, John Daly inhabits, in every conceivable way, that unpredictable, unmanicured terrain far beyond the fairway. It's evident in his disregard for convention. It's obvious from his physique, which is not the lanky body type of so many tour players. It's implicit in the way his long hair once stood out among his well-shorn colleagues. And it's most apparent in his swing, which is not the robotically precise, smooth, easy swing so familiar on the tour, but rather a swing born of pure power and rage, with all the stops pulled out, without self-consciousness or conservatism or concern for its consequences, a swing that ripples through his entire body the way a trumpet solo rippled through and possessed Miles Davis.

Daly is a raw, unrefined kid who hasn't learned—or just doesn't care about—proper etiquette and the quiet, understated demeanor of his fellow pros. He is golf's Charles Barkley; he is its Crazy Cloud Master living in a metaphorical tree house by himself, possibly unaware of his own influence as a teacher of Eastern golf—perhaps unaware, even, of the very Eastern dimension he expresses so purely. The unmanicured instinct that led him to launch that shot out over the crowd at the Fred Meyer Challenge was an expression of pure freedom and individualism and transcendence (all of which are aspects of Zen golf), and exactly what the game needs, in spite of how irresponsible the particular action was. Fans want to be excited and surprised. They crave emotional release: It's what compels them to scream, "You the man!" Fans have had to contain their own feelings and remain silent during professional golf for far too long. Now they want exhilaration and revelation, and the game must provide it in whatever ways it can before these fans turn elsewhere. As my friend Jim Colell explains it, "Golf fans go 'ooh' after every shot because they really just *want* to go 'ooh.' "

John Daly's character is not only wild, it is also deep and genuine. At the Challenge, I watched him on the practice range one morning as he warmed up through all his irons and worked up to hitting his driver. He was actually swinging the club easily until Arnold Palmer came into the practice area and walked toward him. Daly saw Palmer approaching, and began wielding the club with far more vigor, as if to impress Palmer, to win his approval the way a son might look up to his father, the way a novice monk might look up to his teacher. Daly is human, vulnerable, completely real. And his problems with alcohol and in his relationships make him even easier to relate to—especially in comparison to the other bland, perfectly groomed, and honey-voiced pros who seem indistinguishable as they answer interviewers' shallow questions week after week on TV. Though he might not have attained the level of enlightenment of some touring pros, so many fans love Daly best among the many golfers on tour because he is so purely himself.

Peter Jacobsen says of Daly, "There hasn't been this much excitement about a player in years. He's brash and wild and he's a long hitter and people just love him. The best way I can describe it is with that great [mis]quote from *Golf in the Kingdom*: he represents 'the flight from the known to the unknown.'" If Daly can mature without sacrificing his bronclike spirit, if he's willing to recognize and accept the potential power he has to teach us about the deeper aspects of the game, he holds tremendous promise not only as a player but as the kind of individual who can keep the excitement in professional golf.

Beyond the question of why golf fans love John Daly, however, lies the more basic question of why professional golf attracts so many devoted fans to begin with—especially considering that in a five-hour round, pros may actually play the physical part of the sport for less than ten minutes, and there aren't even any opponents trying to tackle them between shots.

Golf tournaments will always draw the serious recreational golfer, who can watch the match as a sort of philosophical spectator sport and who might see it as a koan with the power to reveal secret depths. Since much of the action of professional golf actually occurs inside the players and involves nerves, invisible rhythms, and what the players think about, golf fans must look beyond appearances. They must notice the tiniest nuances of grip, stance, club selection, and pre-shot routine, and interpret these details as if they were full of implicit meaning and potential revelation not only about the game itself but about the world beyond it as well.

These same fans may also watch tournament golf to experience those moments when the action is purely kinetic—undetermined because a ball is still in flight, but simultaneously predetermined, too, because it's already been struck, and there is only the process now, the waiting. During such moments past, present, and future meld into one, as when a putt rolls slowly toward the hole, breaking, breaking, leaning, and you can't determine if it will drop, and you live inside that suspense and time stands still.

These spectators may also spend hours at the practice range watching the pros warm up, the same way that racing aficionados might visit the Thoroughbreds in the paddock before a race. Truly focused fans can pick up the minute variations in mechanics between the pros while noting how any given pro rarely varies from his own particular, individualistic form.

In the several hours I spent watching tournament players at the range before the Challenge, I noticed a great number of revealing details. For example, after finishing their swings, many pros seem more interested in the process—in how their body moved and where their shoulders turned to, and how their legs finished—than in the result of their shot. As true Masters, they know to focus on the journey rather than on the destination, which, if the path is pure, takes care of itself. This was evidenced by the fact that the range's practice greens—even those 250 yards out—were crowded with golf balls, whereas the mass of terrain between them contained a relatively small number of balls. And when ten or twelve players were at the range together, they also watched each other, and discussed the golf swing as a thing of immeasurable beauty, like students comparing opinions on a particularly complex and beautiful passage of text. It's hard to imagine other athletes—baseball players, for example—doing the same.

Zen spectating is a highly developed art, but is probably practiced by a very small part of golf's potential audience. So while serious fans will always show up at tournaments, professional golf must offer something to less evolved viewers as well to bring them into the fold. Such spectators may eventually discover deeper levels of viewing, but to do so, they must find something worth watching in order to bring them out in the first place—such as players interacting with each other and with the fans themselves, communicating some of the joy and mystery and emotion of the game.

The Fred Meyer Challenge is exactly the kind of event that draws people to golf, because it succeeds in conveying the fun and inner character of the sport and its athletes more than any tour event. Maybe it's partly because the Challenge creates less pressure on the pros (and offers far less prize money) than the PGA Championship or the U.S. Open, but it's also because of Peter Jacobsen, one of the most endearing, goofiest, and multitalented players/Masters on the tour. He also happens to possess a personality. Once less-enlightened spectators are drawn to the game because attending a tournament makes for an enjoyable afternoon, they may very well begin to realize there's so much more depth to the sport, and they may begin to pursue those deeper levels.

Peter's Party, as locals refer to the entire three-day event, combines fantastic golf in a dramatic setting, big-name pros, originality, profound silliness, wild parties, emotional earnestness, spontaneity, and an unmanicured approach to tournament play and to life in general. For example, instead of awarding an ugly green sport coat (or an ugly plaid one) to the winners, Jacobsen presents Challenge champions with a sharply styled denim jacket that could make even Jack Nicklaus look almost hip. The event offers up golf as serious sport, but considers sport an occasion for serious fun; even the participants relax enough to be themselves, giving the fans a chance to discover that beyond their generally blond good looks, some pro golfers may actually be human. I've heard several pros remark that they don't come to the Challenge for the money (although they're guaranteed $22,500 plus expenses just for showing up), but because they have such a good time at the event.

For spectators, the pleasure begins as you drive up to the Oregon Golf Club through pine forests and rolling hills, past wild blackberries growing by the roadside and intermittent glimpses of the Willamette River glinting in the sun far below. When you pull into the main gate, the music of homegrown, nationally known jazz artist Tom Grant dances across the landscape, and the golf course itself first appears, winding through forests and ravines and across high, flat summits. Beyond, in the blue distance, the white triangular peak of Mt. Hood floats above the clubhouse, and the rest of the Cascade range forms a gentle horizon line.

As you walk up toward the entrance from the parking lot, good-looking college kids hand out free programs from the *Oregonian*, as well as sports bottles, periscopes, can holders, and other merchandise that could just as easily have been sold as souvenirs. Inside, beyond the gear tents and food courts, the bandstand and dance floor, and the putting and chipping contests, the golf course itself draws you forward.

The layout of the Oregon Golf Club—the first course that Peter Jacobsen designed—is a further tribute to his Masterly talents. At just under 6,800 yards, the par-71 course was built on the sides and summit of a mountain, like a Tibetan monastery. It rolls up and down steep slopes between fast-moving brooks, glass-smooth lakes, wildflower meadows, and thick stands of fragrant pine and Douglas fir. Some holes hang directly above others on the mountainside; the dramatic tenth encourages golfers to risk severe consequences for the reward of hitting the par-four's green on the tee shot if they can clear the tops of some very tall trees.

Most fans arrive early at the Challenge and head right to the eighteenth green to watch the golf clinic and revue that Peter runs on the first two mornings of the event. These hour-long celebrations of the game are precisely what excites even casual spectators and lends them the radical notion that a golf tournament might be fun. The clinics are full of exactly the kinds of revelations that the pros should offer to their eager disciples all the time.

John Daly took his memorable shot at the radio tower during the first morning's golf revue, but that was only a fraction of the wild antics and Masterly offerings that took place. Peter brought out a variety of pros and celebrities for demonstrations and discussions about golf, and he talked about his own life in the game—how he learned to aim a golf shot by trying to hit that little car that retrieves balls at the driving range, and how in high school he was the kind of kid who sat at home in the evenings cleaning the grooves of his clubs.

On that first morning, Jacobsen brought out Jack Lemmon (whom Peter introduced as "the human hinge"), who joked around and hit a few shots. A regular guest at the Challenge, Lemmon admitted to the audience that he was always more nervous on the tee at the Pebble Beach pro-am than he ever was on Broadway. He also told John Daly, who was standing next to him, to "stop sucking around for tips."

Jacobsen then offered some helpful advice to spectators about such matters as gripping the club lightly, keeping the swing in tempo, and perfecting the short game, because the pros really make their money from inside of a hundred yards. He concluded the morning's workshop with his impressions of tour players such as Lanny Wadkins, Arnold Palmer, Tom Kite, and Craig Stadler. For this last one, he poured two buckets of golf balls down his shirt to simulate a huge, waving belly before storming around the stage in mock anger, kicking at his clubs.

On the morning of the second clinic, Jacobsen gave the pros an opportunity to show off their own skills and talk about their games in precisely the way that, as Masters, they should do naturally. To teach the fans a little bit about putting, for example, Peter brought out Rocco Mediate, Bruce

Lietzke, Ben Crenshaw, and Brad Faxon, four of the best putters on the tour. Talking about his own stroke, Crenshaw described in a strangely Zen-like manner how he always putts better without a hole. Then Peter asked Lietzke and Mediate, who use long putters, to switch with Crenshaw and Faxon, who use short ones, so they could stage a little competition—the results of which were hilarious, if inconclusive.

Later in the program, after Daly and Fred Couples and Davis Love demonstrated long drives, Billy Andrade and Tom Kite punched some wedges at one of the sponsors' billboards, and a few other pros showed off, discussed their own specialties, and answered questions from the audience.

There was almost a sense of illicitness in watching the twenty-four tour players joking with each other and with the fans, and having what seemed like way too much fun for a golf tournament. I glanced around to make sure that no PGA Tour officials were taking notes and figuring how many fines to mete out. Looking at the laughing fans gathered on those grassy slopes, you'd never have guessed that they were watching a bunch of normally stiff, short-haired white guys in mostly bad slacks, and learning so much from what they had to say. And if some of what these fans learned contained subliminal Zen overtones, then the lessons were that much more transcendent.

"The true meaning of the precepts," [Bassui] declared enigmatically, "is that one should refrain not only from drinking alcohol but also from getting drunk on nirvana." Then, on one memorable occasion, he openly got drunk in front of all his students, and, when questioned about it, said it was to show them how not to get stuck on regulations!

—*Perle Besserman and Manfred Steger,*
Crazy Clouds: Zen Radicals, Rebels, and Reformers

Not only the mood of the Fred Meyer Challenge but also the actual tournament format encourages an unusual amount of interaction between the players—something fans really respond to. The Challenge employs a team format (which doesn't exist on the tour) where players are paired up into twelve two-man teams; although every pro always plays out his own ball, partners take the better of their two scores on each hole. This not only encourages the pros to talk to each other about shots and strategy, but also to take more chances—which adds a dimension of excitement and uncertainty to the match and a fresh approach to this usually individualistic game, proving that even when you think you've clearly perceived the true nature of golf and placed it into a clear box, you might still discover new ways of seeing it.

I asked several pros what they thought of the format, and they all seemed to like the idea of golf as a team sport, especially as they're so accustomed to being alone out on the course during competition. Arnold Palmer told me, "You have a whole different attitude about your shots. If your partner is in there, you take riskier shots than you normally would."

Steve Elkington, who won the 1993 Fred Meyer with partner Tom Purtzer, said, "The team format puts *more* pressure on because you're playing for your partner as well and you don't want to let him down. You're also more pumped, more into it emotionally than on your own, with the high-fives and the pats on the back." Anything that can make the players feel

197

more emotionally into their matches is certainly good for golf, and will excite the fans.

In so many ways, the Challenge is about as characteristic of professional golf as John Daly is of pro golfers. The event takes tournament play into the unmanicured terrain where the future of golf as a spectator sport lies hidden. If professional golf played in the middle of the fairway is a predictable and sedentary event that only true aficionados can enjoy (unless you find that the gently whispered commentary is the perfect sedative to encourage a Sunday afternoon nap), this tournament represents what pro golf could be outside the strict borders defined by the PGA Tour. Which is great for Zen spectators, and an excellent way of attracting new fans to the game.

In fairness, though, in the same way that many more players than just John Daly and Peter Jacobsen do occasionally demonstrate some personality on the links and live up to their roles as true Masters, the PGA Tour successfully promotes the game in spite of its starched and boringly spiffy and shallow image. Which is to say the tour alone doesn't deserve all the blame for the sedentary nature of tour events. Many journalists who regularly cover professional golf have conspired to relieve the PGA Tour of a good share of that burden.

Aren't you just the slightest bit tired of reading shot-by-shot accounts of a hundred golf tournaments, or those repetitious, recycled instructional articles with titles like ''Three New Short-Game Techniques,'' ''Grip This and Stance That,'' ''Graphite Schmaphite''? And aren't you weary of some golf magazines complaining about how dull the tour is when they won't write about anything beyond the obvious fairway of the game, when they won't ever consider the deep heart of golf, the spiritual side, which is why we all play the sport to begin with?

Sports journalists have a responsibility both to report what happens and to penetrate events and statistics; they must provide readers with a map for exploration and discovery. Golf journalists should be explaining, interpreting, and commenting upon the Masters' lessons, and shedding light on the deeper truths that the pros are teaching us. Because in pursuing the universal truths of Zen and golf, we need the guidance of the Masters. But rather than taking this risk they focus instead on the surface level of the game. When Arnold Palmer sat down in the press room at the Fred Meyer Challenge to answer questions for a few minutes, one local golf writer actually asked the most famous golfer ever to play the game—the winner of more than sixty professional tournaments—how the hills at the Oregon Golf Club compared with other hills he'd played on.

When more of the media, also, begin acknowledging and exploring the unmanicured terrain beyond the fairway of professional golf, the game will resonate with far more meaning and express its true, deep, and irresistible core. Those things that lie buried will rise to the surface where fans and pros alike can articulate them and talk about what golf is really about, why we play it and watch it, what it means to us, and why you shouldn't press the remote control every time the Masters appear on the TV.

CHAPTER THIRTEEN

Golf in the Empire (State)

When the student is ready, the Master appears.
—*Zen saying*

Furthermore, we need an experienced guide to
show us exactly how to put the teachings we
receive into practice. We will not get anywhere if
we try to learn from a book, hoping to figure
things out by ourselves. The . . . texts are
cryptic, revealing their meaning only when
studied together with the explanations of a skilled
practitioner, and it is not easy to know just how
to go about implementing this information. We
need someone to show us, to give us a practical
demonstration. This person is the guru.
—*Lama Thubten Yeshe,* Introduction to Tantra

PETER MARTIN IS STANDING BEHIND A MAN NAMED RED WITH his arms around him, explaining the golf swing in a relaxed, hands-on manner, in a deep, slow, calming voice.

"The *dog* has to wag the *tail,* Red," Martin tells him. "Don't let the *tail* wag the *dog.*"

In this metaphor, Red's body is the dog and his seven iron is the tail. When swinging properly he'll pull the club through the swing with his torso rather than letting the club get out in front, where it can "wag" him.

The metaphor is not particularly original, and Peter Martin is not as obvious a golf Master as John Daly or Peter Jacobsen, but the moment that Martin finishes explaining the concept, and before Red even has the chance to try another swing, a gold-and-white border collie hurries past the practice area, wagging his tail. Student and teacher glance up for only a moment, as if they expected this, before turning back to their lesson.

Such is the implicitly mystical, synchronistic power of Peter Martin's unmanicured golf instruction, the theories of which are based in Eastern philosophies, but take their form from his own hard-core physical, mental, and spiritual discipline. To him, golf can be a form of worship, a system of beliefs that offers up revelations to those who pursue it with strict dedication, pure effort, passion, and the oversight of the right teacher or guide. More important, Martin—a Master in his own right—is teaching what he knows. Although the instruction he offers does not always communicate these hidden aspects of the game directly, such aspects underlie his own experiences and are transferred as a kind of subtext, beyond the obvious fairway of his instruction. The dog that walked past him and Red on the practice range may have been an outward manifestation of that subtext, a corporeal expression of that deeper spirituality.

On the other hand, it might have been chasing a squirrel.

"My friends," he said, "devoted discipline and grace will bring ye knowin's and powers everywhere, in all your life, in all your works if they're good works, in all your loves if they're good loves. Ye'll come away from the links with a new hold on life, that is certain if ye play the game with all your heart."
—*Michael Murphy,* Golf in the Kingdom

Enlightenment, the personal experience of Reality, is man's ultimate experience. The quest for this experience is the most difficult quest upon which he can embark. It demands of him faith, determination, sacrifice, and, above all, passion. Without the sustained sense of urgency which passion imparts, the goal cannot be achieved.
—*Isshu Miura and Ruth Fuller Sasaki,* The Zen Koan

There is more to becoming a great golfer than pursuing the fundamentals, even under the instruction of the best teacher. Unfortunately, some of us possess more innate golf ability than others, and so we may face limits on exactly how far our game can progress. There will always be touring pros, club and resort pros, driving range pros, and various levels of amateurs ranging from talented recreational players to unteachable hackers. However, the true goal of Eastern golfing is to become our own Masters, to attain the highest possible level that we have the capacity to attain. While it may manifest itself through varying degrees of golf Mastery, inner enlightenment is accessible to us all. Following Eastern golf precepts may not land us in a PGA Tour event, but through them we might become the best golfers we can become, and in the process attain even the highest level of enlightenment.

We will not accomplish this kind of dramatic growth by reading and studying either instructional golf books or Eastern philosophy, or by taking a few lessons. A major tenet of Eastern concepts is that we learn the Way through every experience in our lives; but aggressively pursuing a particular discipline, such as archery or golf, may provide a clearer and more direct path. If you choose golf, several things may prove helpful along the way.

Pursuits such as archery and golf may be called disciplines because that's exactly what they require—not simply perseverance, but true dedication and commitment. But even with discipline, tremendous growth is unlikely without abiding passion. And even with both passion and discipline, we may still require the input of a great teacher to help us on our journey.

Peter Martin is the PGA professional and golf instructor at the Whiteface Inn Resort and Club, just outside of Lake Placid, New York, and is one such Master. A former professor and Ph.D. candidate in philosophy at the University of Colorado, he's a cross between characters from *Golf in the Kingdom* and Plato's *Republic*. Tall and thin, with swanlike grace, short graying hair, and a mustache, he'd seem perfectly comfortable in a toga discussing subjects ranging from par threes to Parmenides, from Anaxagoras to Seve Ballesteros.

Many years ago, just short of earning his doctorate, Martin was out walking in the Rocky Mountains when he realized that he didn't really want his academic degree. So he climbed into his car and drove to Florida without even retrieving his belongings, which he claims didn't amount to much, anyway. Soon after, he began a career in golf that has allowed him to pursue and profess philosophy in a far more direct and less esoteric way than he ever could have in a university classroom. Martin currently incorporates the fundamentals of yoga, asceticism, Zen, Eastern mysticism, and other teachings in his golf instruction and in his own game, and he insists that golf can be as much of a discipline as philosophy or religion. By studying the game with the right attitude, with passion, and with patience and humility, devoted students may not only ascend to higher planes of existence, but may simultaneously correct any tendency toward shanking their irons as well.

As evidence that Martin's theories work, you need only look at Red, who by the end of his half-hour lesson was swinging dramatically slower and more accurately. He'd shortened and narrowed his stance, and had relaxed almost to the point of semiconsciousness. When Martin told him to hit the few remaining practice balls at the eighteenth green, Red dropped nearly every one of them on the putting surface with his seven iron. He nodded in self-approval, as if he'd just gotten back a term paper on existentialism with a bright red A+ scrawled across the top of the first page.

The Head Pro and one of his private students were playing the golf course late in the afternoon of an autumn day. Wondering how much longer into the season they might be able to continue the lessons, the student asked, "What happens when the leaves are falling, and the trees are bare?"

The Head Pro replied, "The golden wind, revealed."
                                        —*Zen golf koan*

The Whiteface Inn's golf course and even the resort's geographical location accurately reflect Peter Martin's own personality and teaching style: serene, quirky, and far removed from the obvious fairway of resort golf and golf instruction. The property is tucked away deep in New York State's Adirondack Mountains—good, old-fashioned, largely undeveloped mountains speckled with lakes and trout streams, a place where the trees turn every imaginable shade of orange, red, yellow, and brown in the crisp autumns. In fact, what I remember best about meeting Martin for the first time one fall was the way he reached up with one hand as he drove our cart over the rutted paths and smooth fairways of the golf course, trying to catch bright, flaming leaves as they fell from the sugar maples.

Although remote, the Adirondacks have a well-established golf history. In the late nineteenth and early twentieth centuries, Scottish golf course architects such as Donald Ross, Seymour and Willie Dunn, and Alex Findlay built layouts beside the grand hotels that drew wealthy urbanites to these mountains from throughout the Northeast. In recent decades, many of the old hotels and golf courses have disappeared back into the wilderness, but Martin has preserved their memory in an excellent golf history book he wrote, entitled *Adirondack Golf Courses Past and Present*.

Luckily for visiting golfers, the rugged golf layout at the Whiteface Inn survived. Perched on the edge of Lake Placid, the course was redesigned by Walter Hagen and John Van Kleek in 1930, and offers a wild, backcountry golf experience. The holes wind through hardwood forests of pine, maple, fir, and birch that you almost want to hit into just for the pleasure of walking through. The layout exudes an out-of-season spaciousness even in summer. The views of the Adirondack high peaks will make you feel as if you're a thousand miles—and as many years—from the hurry of the real world. And a few golf lessons with Peter Martin will reinforce the sense that you've stepped out of that world for a while, into a strange, resonant place where golf and philosophy merge into a single pursuit, at the heart of which lies the possibility of revelation.

Martin's basic golf philosophy is simple. He believes the game consists of three distinct levels—physical, mental, and spiritual—that form a logical hierarchy. Some students may progress from the first to the third, but many golfers never advance beyond the first stage, because ascension requires discipline, hard work, and the vision to see beyond the ordinary surface of the game.

In Peter Martin's universe, you must first master the basics of the game, and the basics are physical. As Martin explains, "Big Bertha won't make you a better golfer. I see some guys who expect this when they can hardly even climb out of their cars. In fact, we know more about how our cars work than about how our bodies work."

To get in touch with our own physicality, and to prepare our bodies for golf, Martin advocates both stretching and building the appropriate muscles. "If you're not getting anywhere in your game, perhaps you haven't earned it yet," he says. "Paying your dues physically gives you the freedom to go beyond the basic level.'' More specifically, dues paying may involve stretching out essential muscles such as the hamstrings and lower back, performing isometric exercises, and lifting weights to strengthen the arms and hands.

Once a golfer has worked his body into shape to play golf, he may be ready to address the mental part of the game. Martin, who believes that tension is the greatest enemy of the golf swing, advocates relaxation techniques such as deep breathing and visualization to help set the mind at ease. A relaxed player, and one who understands, for example, that his golf ball actually goes where he hits it, will not get tense and angry when a shot misses the target.

The mental game also involves overcoming fears and misconceptions. While I was golfing with Martin, he encouraged me not to hit short on my approach shots. ''It's hard to think about hitting beyond the flag because we don't know what's there,'' he reflected. ''We're afraid of the unknown. Especially since the flags are often red, and that sends a particular message—a red flag.''

When a golfer has worked his way up through both the physical and mental challenges of the game, he may be ready to begin climbing toward the third level, the spiritual, where golf segues into philosophy. Peter Martin loves to work with golfers who've reached stage two but aren't even fully aware that stage three exists. He says, ''Many players are afraid to admit that they don't know how to take the next step, as if not knowing is a sign of weakness. But you have to give up ego attachment, and often you need help. I'm the guide who can take you up that mountain.''

As in yoga and many other Eastern systems of belief, balance also occupies an important place in the Eastern golf philosophy, not only *within* each of the three levels of the golf game, but *between* them as well. Martin himself seeks balance in all areas of his life, from diet and exercise to the music he listens to.

All of these aspects of the game require strict discipline and recognition of the fact that the work is never complete. Learning golf—or any other system—involves a journey, and that journey, as we know by now, is actually its own goal. No shortcuts exist because the destination is the exploration itself, and therefore getting there any faster or with less effort is impossible.

Peter Martin is a dedicated practitioner of his own theories, and although his golf game ascended to a high level a long time ago, he still rigorously pursues the basics. A marathon runner and triathlete at age fifty, he's fanatical about working out aerobically nearly every day, whether he goes running through the woods, swimming in the lake behind the resort, or riding his bike along local country roads. He also performs stretching and strengthening exercises religiously every evening. "Golf isn't a cross between badminton and croquet," he claims. "You're swinging the club a hundred miles an hour and you need strength and flexibility."

Martin first began this exercise program not out of some philosophical principle, but out of pure physical necessity. After injuring his back while skiing one winter (he's another pro who appears to have recognized the intrinsic connections between these two sports), the only way he could golf pain-free was by limbering up—and not just for five minutes before a round. But he soon discovered that stretching and other physical disciplines provided a means of accessing a higher realm.

In addition to his exercise regimen, Martin maintains a rigorous caffeine-free vegetarian diet. When he was training for the Boston Marathon a number of years ago, he even took to eating mostly plain bowls of rice—without using utensils—because he enjoyed the ascetic purity of it. To that end, he also fasts occasionally to cleanse his system and because he likes the way it feels. "There can't be any spiritual enlightenment until there's physical enlightenment," he explains.

As for mental and spiritual discipline, Martin pursues these aspects of enlightenment privately but no less vigorously. For example, he practices deep breathing whenever he feels a need for it, and he and his wife occasionally perform "deep singing" to help them relax. And Martin still reads everything he can find on the subject of mysticism, and follows the specific spiritual teachings of a particular Master of yoga.

Martin's own passion is evident in the way he talks about golf and spiritualism, in the excitement with which he plays golf and pursues his enlightenment, and in the fact that he's dedicated himself wholly to these pursuits: They are not hobbies, but rather his life's work.

Many golfers will not care to hear about this particular approach to golf. Members of what I call the school of gear-and-gimmick golfers, for example, won't believe in such things as passion and discipline, because that would mean letting go of their belief that you can easily and permanently correct whatever's wrong with your golf game by discovering the right shortcut. The gear-and-gimmick player buys a lot of new golf clubs—Big Bertha, the White Whale, the Fire Stick, the Triceratops, the Valkyrie on Steroids—figuring such high-tech equipment possesses some kind of intrinsic magic independent of his ability to swing it. Or he picks up a tip from a magazine or TV (or from some guy at the club who's worse than he is), certain he's finally found the one thing that will fix his game. But what kind of deep, true meaning could golf really possess if Mastery resided in owning the right equipment rather than inside the player himself, if any lazy dilettante could simply spend the money to purchase a respectable game the way rich men once bought salvation from the Church?

For the past six months, my father—who is neither lazy nor a dilettante, and who is as passionate about golf as anyone I know—has been setting up in his golf stance with his back foot bent as if he'd come down on it wrong and broken his ankle. This twisted posture is supposed to prevent him from backing away from the ball in his downswing, which he's been doing for the past thirty-five or forty years. My father paid perfectly good money for the lesson that included this potentially metamorphosing tip, yet he still refuses to go out and practice even this shortcut, let alone anything else he's ever learned about the golf swing. And he's frustrated because he's taken private lessons and been to golf school, and he owns a set of Pings, but his game just doesn't improve.

When I tell him as gently as I can—suppressing my desire to scream and threaten him with a fairway wood—that by hitting a small bucket of balls before every round he could probably take five strokes off his game and maybe even correct some of his long-term problems, he appears to have a bit of trouble with his hearing. I guess he figures that he's paid for his improved swing in hard currency, so why should he have to expend time and effort as well? In spite of the fact that golf is one of the most important things in my father's life, and that he's been playing rather badly for several decades, it's still not worth it to him to pay his dues and approach the game with even the slightest amount of discipline. If my father were one of Peter Martin's students, he would probably be left back.

He has plenty of passion, but lacks discipline.

At the opposite extreme, I had a friend in college who was fanatical about practicing his golf swing: Each morning before class (or sometimes instead of class) he stood in front of a mirror working on his form. He pounded balls at the driving range whenever he could. He pitched on the lawn in front of his dorm. He putted on the rug in his room, aiming between books and pizza boxes and empty beer cans. On the golf course, he severely criticized every mistake of form or execution that he committed, and reminded himself of the correct principles. Playing golf with him was like spending the day with a military dictator, because he never enjoyed himself, never really felt a genuine passion for the game. He seemed to have some ulterior motive for pursuing golf so relentlessly—perhaps to impress his friends, or to ease parental pressure, or to defeat some of the other very competitive players in our group. He didn't love the game for itself, but saw it as a way of accomplishing something of far less spiritual value. To him, golf was a means toward an end, not its own reward. Which goes to prove that discipline by itself, without an accompanying passion, is not enough, either.

Many of these tenets of the Eastern path to golf Mastery became clear to me during and after a weekend I spent with Peter Martin, in the course of which he explained much of his golf philosophy, both out on the course and over dinner at his home along the sixteenth hole at Whiteface Inn.

During the season, Martin lives with his beautiful wife, An-

211

noel, in the dark, old, original clubhouse. (In appropriate yin-yang balance, they live beside a *light*house in South Carolina during winter.) Before eating, as we drank cold cans of Foster's beer—which Martin refers to as the bad habit he needs to balance out all of his discipline—he showed me the office where he's begun the preliminary work on a book about his theories of golf. The room failed to reflect any of the order and control so obvious in his thinking. It was amazingly cluttered with old wagon wheels, modern and antique golf clubs, worn socks, five or six pairs of running shoes, and two or three pairs of golf shoes; every surface was covered with notepads, folders stuffed with articles on yoga or lists of back exercises, or old magazines; and the walls were hung with golf photographs, tournament announcements, newspaper clippings about Martin and every other conceivable subject related to golf in any way, charts of the human muscle groups, a schedule for National Public Radio programs, and hastily scribbled notes that Martin had written to himself: "Patience is control," and "The spirit must be tapped." On one bookshelf I noticed the titles of two well-thumbed volumes: *Zen, Drugs, and Mysticism,* and *Yoga Self-Taught.*

Over dinner, Martin and Annoel and I discussed a dizzying variety of topics, including the nature of art, the spirit of golf, music, travel, spiritualism, outdoor recreation, skiing, log cabins, bartending, and LSD trips. In the background a composite tape of Leonard Cohen, Paul Horn, George Winston, and other soothing, eerie New Age tunes floated through the dark wood house as candles flickered and our voices grew excited and then soft again.

Whenever we returned to the subject of his own golf philosophy—which I tried to do often—Martin spoke slowly and carefully and sometimes inarticulately. When I asked him about yoga, for example, which is a kind of religion for him as well as something that resides at the heart of his theories about golf, he admitted that this was a rather private issue. He called yoga "a way of knowing God," and explained that his stretching and other aspects of his life are simply outward manifestations of that process. He also told me that many years ago, when he thought he knew a lot about philosophy, spiritualism, and golf, yoga showed him that he really knew virtually nothing at all.

Martin's hesitance to discuss the inner game too explicitly may be a consequence of his beliefs, which lead him to question whether he's really learned enough to be espousing his thoughts to others. He is a cautious, reticent Master. His is a humble sort of enlightenment, and though a particular path has worked for him, he doesn't necessarily advocate that same path for others. As he put it, "When the physical and mental aspects are in place, the spiritual follows. But people have to find their own definitions for what this means. They have to find their own gods. God is inside. You see God when climbing a mountain or running the twenty-fourth mile of a marathon. You see your limits as further than you thought you could go. This often requires living a life full of compassion, understanding, sympathy, tolerance, and forgiveness."

Though we spoke animatedly for hours about these concepts, I recall few specifics of what Martin said. But I do remember the subtext, and how right much of our conversation felt, as if he and Annoel and I were somehow communicating beyond words, which did not have the capacity to express what we meant.

I also intuited much of Martin's philosophy on the golf course, communicated through his metaphors and through the soft, gentle voice he used to explain aspects of the swing to me. On the final day of my visit, he took me out to the nearby Saranac Inn golf course, a Seymour Dunn layout where Martin had caddied as a teenager. As an experiment, I barely ate anything that entire day, just to see whether I'd experience any of the heightened ascetic awareness that Martin attributed to fasting. Hemingway felt the same way about his writing—that a writer should work with the edge of hunger driving him.

Whether it was my hunger, the perfect, clear, warm afternoon, or the modifications that Martin made in my swing throughout the day, I shot an 86 from the blue tees—a good score for me considering that I hadn't played golf in a month and that it was my first time on that course. I also won seventy-five cents from my teacher.

Much of his Masterly advice to me was specific rather than philosophical, although it came in the form of analogies. He told me, for example, to imagine while in the top of my backswing that I was a waiter carrying a tray of drinks. The downswing, however, should feel like a doctor slapping a newborn baby. As he put it, "The secret to the downswing is knowing when to use the right hand in the hitting zone—those fifteen inches before and after impact—the way a doctor slaps a newborn on the butt."

Martin also worked on my approach and setup and my golf posture. He encouraged me to tee the ball farther forward in my stance, and stand closer to it. He opened my front foot and showed me how to set the club face at a perfect ninety-degree angle to the line between my feet and the ball. He explained that the legs are the pillars of the swing and all energy rises up through them, and that I needed to stay in balance at all times. He recommended posing, as if for a photo, as I finished my follow-through.

He also offered an interesting perspective on perception by explaining that very often the last thing we look at before addressing the ball is the object we end up hitting toward. So, for instance, if there's a golf cart off to your left in the rough, and you glance at it one last time just to make sure it's out of range before swinging at the ball, you're likely to hit in exactly that direction.

By the end of the day, I understood clearly that although everything Peter Martin practices, believes in, and teaches about golf has a basis in Eastern philosophy and other esoteric subjects, these things are often completely invisible in his teaching—as subtext always is. He is deeply *passionate* and solidly *disciplined* on his individualistic path to enlightenment and golf Mastery, and in his teaching, and those are among the most important things he passed along to me. If I had to describe his method of instruction, I would say that—as in Zen—there was no dogma at all. Only doglegs, and dogs wagging their tails.

PART FOUR

East of Beyond:
Enlightenment at the
Game's Unmanicured
Outer Limits

———

CHAPTER FOURTEEN

Thai Score

At a gathering of all of his assistants, the Head Pro picked up a flower he'd taken from the border garden planted around the putting green, and showed it to the group.

Everyone was silent and still except for assistant pro Kashyapa, who broke out in a smile.

The Head Pro said, "I have the treasury of the eye of truth, the ineffable mind of nirvana, the most subtle of teachings on the formlessness of the form of reality. It is not defined in words but is specially transmitted outside of doctrine. I entrust it to assistant pro Kashyapa."

—*Zen golf koan*

We are living in a realm of desire. From the moment we wake up until the moment we fall asleep at night, and throughout our dreams, we are driven by desire. Each of our senses is hungry for its own particular food. Our eye craves to see

219

interesting shapes and colours; our ears want to
hear pleasing sounds; our nose actively sniffs out
agreeable odours . . . ; our tongue seeks exciting
new tastes and our sense of touch is forever
craving contact of one kind or another. This
desire for sensory stimulation is so deeply
ingrained that if we are isolated from sights,
sounds, smells, and so forth for long enough we
begin to hallucinate them.
—*Lama Thubten Yeshe,* Introduction to Tantra

A S MY HIRED CAR CRAWLS ALONG IN TRAFFIC TOWARD THE
Oriental Hotel in Bangkok, Thailand, it seems as if every
last one of the city's six million residents is simultaneously
steering some sort of vehicle along this same route. Yet in
spite of labyrinthine gridlock, blaring horns, clouds of diesel
fumes, careening *tuk-tuks* (small cabs, like tricycles with Boeing
engines), and temperature and humidity both hovering around
one hundred, my chauffeur never demonstrates even the
slightest irritation. In a capital that has earned an unparalleled
reputation for the worst traffic in the world, residents have
developed a driving style that expresses a perfect balance between aggression and politeness—a kind of motorly enlightenment. If this were New York, someone would surely be
dead by now.

When we stop at the same traffic light for the fourth time,
my driver rolls down his window and purchases a garland of
pale yellow jasmine flowers from a vendor calmly conducting
business between rows of cars. When we emerge from traffic—several days from now—the driver intends to place this
garland around the spirit house in his yard as a peaceful offering.

Pondering his tranquillity, and comparing it to my own pounding headache, my sense of impending claustrophobia, my inclination to lean out the window and scream at somebody, I understand implicitly that Thais are true Masters at transporting themselves beyond surface manifestations and somehow finding not only harmony and repose, but pure, aesthetic beauty in virtually any situation. And at the same time, Thais also actively imbue events and activities with just such pleasures—hence a vendor selling flower garlands in the middle of traffic in the first place. This aspect of the so-called Oriental mystique is explicit in a thousand dimensions of Thai life, from the fact that Bangkok boasts hotels (such as the Regent and the Oriental) that consistently rank among the best in the world, to the way Thai restaurants serve a dizzying cornucopia of brightly colored fruits intricately carved into works of art. Every aspect of Thai experience emphasizes and enhances the sensations. Natives delight in the sensuous possibilities of details. They look beyond how things are and consider how they could be. And then they leap to bridge and balance these opposing elements.

Of course, some activities possess more potential for ecstasy than others, which is a reason why Thais so love the game of golf: It is bursting with the splendors of form, shape, color, scent, and sound. Smooth, rolling swaths of greenery wend between the straight, upright lines of trees, giving off the scent of springtime and freshly cut grass; flowers and grasses meld in wild profusion; sand and water create dichotomies of hue and texture; balls blast off with a crisp thwack and land with a deep thud; and the very rhythm and ritual of the game provide deep satisfaction.

In the contrast of two cultures of Buddhism—Zen asceticism (as practiced by Peter Martin, for example) and Thai aestheticism—golfers can experience the wide range of the sport's joys. On the one hand, we can play the Zen game, in which we balance strength with precision, and distance with aim; in which the easier we swing, the farther our ball travels; in which we transcend all the surface tensions and self-consciousness that threaten to clog the pure flow of our play. On the other hand, we can pursue the Thai way, where, regardless of a few botched shots, we can still focus on the deeper enjoyment of our swing, the ball in motion, and the way the yellow flag stands out against the deep green grass, transforming these small moments of beauty into a means of attaining larger universal truths.

I first began to understand these principles while I was lining up a long putt on the sweltering ninth hole of the Rose Garden Golf Course, just outside Bangkok, a few hours before drifting into that endless loop of city traffic. As I read the break of the perfectly manicured green, a glint of silver advancing toward me from the clubhouse caught my eye. Was it a heat mirage? Someone's Rolex reflecting sunlight? A UFO?

I felt a bit loopy from the heat, but could have sworn that a well-dressed servant was approaching with a silver tray full of chilled towels and tall glasses of iced tea.

I turned to my two caddies. One carried my clubs while the other toted a huge umbrella to shield me from the sun. Both were young, pretty women.

"Am I *dreaming*," I wondered?

The caddies nodded and smiled as I drained the putt for my par and reached for an icy drink.

My hosts at the Rose Garden imbued my entire day with such delights: a lunch—held in the cool, spacious VIP dining room overlooking the golf course—of airy tempura, fresh sushi, and cold beer; a pile of T-shirts, hats, gloves, and other items from the pro shop; and a chance to play eighteen holes with Puchong Yuvaboon, the owner of the resort, and Visudh Junenanonda, the architect who designed the golf course.

The course itself expresses Mr. Visudh's own personal vision of beauty, and features wide, soft fairways sliced by clear streams, buffered by elegant trees, and exploding with tropical flowers. In fact, each hole is named after and decorated with a different brilliantly colorful blossom.

Mr. Visudh informed me that "a tough course creates good golfers," and that he had incorporated this idea as part of his design. I'd always thought a tough course created high blood pressure, but maybe he was right. Based on this philosophy, he created three nearly perfect and exceedingly difficult finishing holes. The eighteenth, in particular, is like a gorgeously worked sculpture: 530 yards departing from an island tee, crossing a stream halfway home, offering views over other water, and decorated with several traps sprinkled pleasingly around the green. All the water hazards are thick with lily pads blossoming into purple lotus flowers, a touch conducive to hours of meditative contemplation.

And just in case the astonishing attraction of the layout isn't enough, the Rose Garden's management staffs every water hazard with a young boy who dives in to retrieve lost balls. If he can't find yours, write down your name and the type of ball you lost, and come back for it the next time you're in the neighborhood. This is another excellent example of the extremes to which the Thais go to ensure a golfer's pleasure.

The Rose Garden course lies just beyond the city limits of Bangkok, which, in terms of *its* overall layout, expresses the frantic entropy of a Jackson Pollack painting—as if generations of city planners had flung buildings randomly at the canvas of downtown. Chrome-and-glass skyscrapers soar beside ancient temples; wooden shacks propped on stilts above the river eclipse modern hotels; American fast-food joints abut a palace-like structure erected in the style of the Italian Renaissance.

Yet, in spite of its unsettling discordance, this complex, bustling city on the Chao Phraya River still manages to convey order and peace, if—like the Thais—you know how to spot it beneath the surface. The pleasing motion of students practicing t'ai chi amid the greenery of Lumpini Park; a water taxi ride through the *klongs* (canals); a pair of barefoot, orange-robed monks with shaven heads wandering through the markets with their polished wooden alms bowls—so many details offer a kind of sensorial serenity. And Bangkok's golf courses, each a respite as pure and peaceful as a private garden shrine, also help to balance the city's frantic activity with leafy, meditative stillness. In Thailand's frenetic capital, golf links serve an essential function.

More than twenty courses lie scattered around the city like calm oases, and each breathes its own moist, photosynthesized spaciousness into the chaotic air. Navatanee Golf Course, designed by Robert Trent Jones, Jr., is adorned by more flowers than a Monet painting—including a particular bloom, called pumaria, which is prohibited inside Thai houses because of its common use at funerals, which might seem appropriate if you have a bad round of golf here. This thinking man's course forces players to look beyond the obvious shots to consider the deeper, more precise elegance of strategy. Architect Jones (ungrammatically) described the thirteenth hole at Navatanee as "a deceivably cute par three requiring a delicate pitch shot." He also modestly called number eighteen "one of the greatest holes in the world of golf." Jones employed two-tiered greens, curvy ponds, and holes that bend and undulate, producing a layout that's extremely pleasing to the eye. Another inadvertent visual touch during my round at Navatanee was a woman in a yellow hat standing in a blue boat tending the green reeds lining one of the water hazards. And adding to the overall character, the clubhouse contains the most attractive phone booths I've ever seen—pyramids of smooth, dark teak that I couldn't resist rubbing my hands over, wishing I had someone to call.

Not far from Navatanee, another course on the outskirts of Bangkok offers its own quite different allure. The Pinehurst Golf Club sports three distinctive and well-balanced nines, each expressing its personality through different elements of design. The West (or Forest) layout emulates an Asian parkland, with thick stands of trees shaping the golf course; the South (or Meadow) course contains the humps and bumps of a Scottish links; and the North (or Lakes) layout resembles the kind of watery course you might find in Michigan. The entire development is ringed by canals and whispery, pinelike casuarina trees. With picturesque bridges, palm trees, and clusters of bright flowers, Pinehurst feels as relaxing as a shiatsu massage.

Nearly every golf course in Thailand also features at least one spirit house, where the golf course spirits may take up residence when the land is disturbed or occupied. Locals drape these intricate miniature pagodas with flower garlands, ribbons, and other multicolored offerings that appease human eyes as well as spirits. It's not a bad idea to leave a little something as you pray for a good iron game.

For Westerners, the only downside to the aspect of peacefulness that permeates Thai golf is that since the game represents a kind of religious ritual, natives like to play slowly, enjoying every golf shot and drinking in every view. Thais sometimes play in groups of five or six, with two caddies per player, so you'll have to get used to seeing battalions of eighteen people occasionally crowding tees and greens. To further decelerate play, most groups stop at each of the snack shacks located every three holes. The best idea is to simply breathe deeply and let go of the notion of finishing the round in time to go shopping in the afternoon. Better to lose yourself in the Thai golfing experience, and see the true beauty of the game as it looks from beyond the fairway.

Although Thais have been playing golf since the beginning of this century, it was when their king took up the game in the 1920s that his subjects really went crazy over it. Soon golf became so popular with members of the royal court that it threatened to interrupt the business of ruling the country. To ensure domestic tranquillity, the king was forced to decree that any of his retinue overheard discussing golf off the course would have to pay a fine.

If at any point you find yourself busy not-golfing in Thailand, make sure to visit the royal palace, which served as the home of Thai kings for two hundred years until one unlucky ruler was murdered inside it in 1946. Every monarch added his own architectural imprint to the grounds, which include styles ranging from indigenous Thai to classical French, mirroring the chaotic diversity of the surrounding city.

On the same grounds, Wat Phra Keo—the Temple of the Emerald Buddha—provides a further example of the Thai emphasis on sensory stimuli by presenting an Oriental fantasyland of shapes and colors, lights and shadows, soothing silence and tinkling bells. Golden spires reach up beyond jade elephants and sculpted topiary. Huge urns house green water lilies blossoming with purple flowers. Incense floats on the breeze and statues ripple with gold leaf rubbed onto them by pious followers. Enormous saber-toothed gods and brightly colored monsters guard entranceways, and the tiles and mirrors decorating the architecture reflect a kaleidoscope of hue and pattern in an overwhelming shower of sensation.

The centerpiece of the temple-and-royal-palace complex is the Emerald Buddha itself (coincidentally the color of a well-tended Bermuda grass fairway), a religious icon that traveled throughout the Far East beginning in the fifteenth century before finding a permanent home in Bangkok. Three times each year, the Thai king changes the Buddha's clothes according to the season, so it will be comfortable.

Tantra recognizes the powerful energy aroused by our desires to be an indispensable resource for the spiritual path . . . tantra seeks to transform every experience— no matter how "unreligious" it may appear—into the path of fulfillment. It is precisely because our present life is so inseparably linked with desire that we must make use of desire's tremendous energy if we wish to transform our life into something transcendental. Thus the logic of tantra is really very simple: our experience of

227

ordinary pleasure can be used as the resource for attaining the supremely pleasurable experience of totality, or enlightenment.

—*Lama Thubten Yeshe*, Introduction to Tantra

Between rounds of golf and visits to palaces and temples, I had the chance to go scuba diving in southern Thailand, off Phuket Island in the Andaman Sea. I discovered that diving not only took the notion of penetrating surfaces to a new level (literally), but that diving and Thai golf share certain subtle characteristics. In fact, diving also involves the same pursuance of an individualistic journey as do golfing and skiing and so many other transcendent I-N-G activities. Underwater, there's really no specific destination—the traveling itself is everything. And, as in tantric tradition, diving is a festival for the senses, which could easily lead toward revelation and enlightenment, not to mention the surprising of many sea creatures.

Describing the intricacy of a living reef is a lot like trying to explain the joys of golf to a person who has never felt the *whoosh-clack* of a perfectly struck seven iron and never watched his white ball rising high into the blue atmosphere before dropping onto the soft, receptive surface of a gently sloping green.

During the initial minutes of a dive, I often feel the same tense self-consciousness that I have to transcend on the first tee of a famous golf course when I'm playing a round with the pro. Early in my first dive off Phuket, I held on to my depth and pressure gauges with a viselike grip and consulted them every other second. I repeated over and over to myself what I had to do: establish neutral buoyancy, breathe slowly, don't bang into any coral, don't go too deep. I felt myself battling the exact kind of panic you try to suppress when you're on the verge of shooting a new personal-best round, but you have to par the toughest hole on the course coming in and you still have plenty of opportunities to screw things up.

But there comes a moment in every dive when all of that self-consciousness falls away. Without warning, as the shadow of the dive boat's hull grew fainter, a blue flash shook me from my introversion. A bright, tiny fish had darted out from his tiny studio apartment in the coral. I glanced around for the first time and suddenly remembered where I was. I discovered myself floating along in an ocean vibrant with activity, at a fantastical party full of strange shapes and colors, much like a bar I'd visited in Bangkok's Patpong district.

Had this hidden world been there all along, beyond the dials and arrows on my gauges? I felt a humble gratitude at being allowed to visit this realm, where everything glowed in fluorescent halos of light and where visibility seemed endless. I smiled. I waved at passing fish. I gave myself up to the nuzzling current and drifted above coral jungles as if in a dream.

I watched as if I were viewing some distant planet inhabited by creatures so bizarre and so magical that they could star in their own science fiction movie: lionfish skimming the sea floor with their poisonous spines undulating in the current, boxfish floating along like brightly wrapped presents, seahorses bobbing on invisible carousels. Looking at the plain and infinite dark surface of the ocean, who would even imagine such a variety of forms existed below?

Coral reefs are a lot like pointillist paintings: When you view them from a distance, you notice large coral heads, rocks, a few chunky fish swimming past. But when you move closer and look beyond obvious appearances, the profusion of microcosmic whorls and patterns is dizzying. You notice that the reef's coral structure consists of many different corals—staghorn and mushroom, leaf and lettuce, fine-spined, foliose, pore. You recognize giant Neptune's cup sponges, plate-shaped blue anemones, green radiata, sea mats, sea slugs, and sea cucumbers. Long-spined and banded sea urchins project sharp purple needles the way the sun projects golden rays of light.

And all around the living architecture, brightly costumed fish dance through this weightless ballroom with the happy abandon of drunks: big fish, such as humpbacked groupers, who swim right up and stare at you with their jowly faces practically begging for a cigar; schools of yellowtail in synchronized motion; snappers; butterfly fish in half a dozen fluttering varieties; eight kinds of angelfish; clown fish wearing silly, self-satisfied pastel grins. Wherever you turn there are fish arcing and orbiting and turning gracefully in a parade of ebony, cerulean, teal, lavender, cerise, in latticed patterns, with bold spots, silhouetted in white, etched with delicate stripes. Parrot fish. Moon wrasses. Electric blue starfish lying back with their arms spread languorously in welcome, like Mae West lounging on a divan in an azure gown.

The depth and variety of sensory experience seems endless once you move beneath the surface. It's like looking up from a difficult sand shot, when all you can see is the bunker itself, and realizing that you're playing Pete Dye's TPC Stadium Course in Florida. You notice that the grass has been sculpted into lovely mounds, the fairways curve gracefully, and the ponds lined with weathered wooden railroad ties are like calm reflecting pools. In the distance, beyond the swaying sawgrass, an island green shimmers beneath the lavender early-evening sky. The sensation is of floating, being borne up and carried along by the spirit of the sport.

A diver penetrates beneath the surface to see colors and shapes, to have unguessed-at experiences. The same kinds of exhilaration are possible in golf when you look beyond the fairway at the endless sensual details.

> Through the practice of tantra all activity motivated by desire—even drinking a milk shake—can be transformed into the experience of great blissful wisdom.
> —*Lama Thubten Yeshe*, Introduction to Tantra

No account of life and golf in Thailand—and particularly of the Thais' emphasis on physical pleasures—would be complete without considering the country's near-religious reverence for food. Always artistically presented in a perfect blend of hues and shapes and textures, Thai food combines fresh meat and shellfish, brightly colored vegetables, and bold Eastern seasonings that will alternately stir up and ease your palate. One night, at the beach resort of Pattaya two hours from Bangkok, my Thai host ordered a meal for me that was nearly too beautiful to eat: *tom yum,* a spicy and milky seafood soup; chicken wrapped in banana leaves; scallops and squid in a chili and pepper sauce; and a swarm of prawns as big as lobsters, which crowded off the plate toward separate hot and sweet dipping sauces. While eating, I became very popular with several waiters, whom I amused with my ability to sweat profusely from the red-hot food.

If Thai meals set your synapses firing, you'll be glad to know that Thailand is blessed with an embarrassing overabundance of cool, soothing fruits with names that sound like they should be outlying provinces: durian, santol, mangosteen, rambutan. The Thais have also perfected frozen fruit drinks such as pineapple and coconut shakes that will bring your temperature down and set your taste buds mamboing with tropical joy.

My excellent and memorable meal in Pattaya preceded what I can only describe as a brief moment of completely serene, aesthetically pure golf—which stands as the perfect representation of my entire visit to Thailand.

I experienced this pure bliss on the sixteenth hole at the Siam Country Club, not far from my cliff-hugging hotel in Pattaya. My golf that day was so bad that I wished I'd brought along a hara-kiri sword as my fourteenth club, to perform the only honorable action left to me. To make things even worse, after I topped an iron shot about thirty yards ahead of me late in the round, my caddy—who hadn't spoken a word all afternoon—turned and said, "No head down," which wouldn't have bothered me so much except that it's what my father says anytime I hit a bad shot.

But the day was still fine and the golf course lovely, nestled among dry hills full of bright green pineapple plantations and somehow reminiscent of the Spanish countryside. I tried to let some of that beauty inside of me. The course itself—a tough, mature layout—drew me along narrow fairways, most of which ran up or down gentle slopes. Many were decorated with a stream meandering by on its unhurried way someplace, and all offered generous, wide-ranging views.

By the late afternoon I was worn down from walking in the heat, and worried about whether I'd finish my round before dark. I was disappointed in my poor play, sleepy, hungry, and feeling pressured to hurry my shots to reach the last few holes.

But then I looked up briefly from the sixteenth tee in time

to see the sun dropping like a ripe fruit through the branches of a fragrant, blossoming, bright orange flame tree, set against a clear backdrop of cobalt sky. I stared toward the horizon as if in a dream, and the air seemed to shimmer before me, the earth to float in a pure and ethereal present.

Suddenly, in a moment of acute harmony and revelation, everything—my golf game, my fears and shortcomings and worries, my hunger, the soreness in my right arm, every thought of insecurity and self-consciousness and doubt—peeled away until nothing was left but a pure, empty core as I watched the flaming sunset. My memories and emotions rose up and merged in continuous flow, and a sense of wholeness I can only describe as transcendent filled me the way rainwater runs to fill an empty stream channel.

While this was happening, I was fully unaware of it in any self-conscious way: It just *was*.

I breathed deeply, and felt my muscles unclenching.

I pulled a club from my golf bag, stepped up on the tee, and released a long, straight shot into the darkening sky without caring—without even a thought about—where it might land.

CHAPTER FIFTEEN

Pilgrim's Progress: Golfing Nepal

Assistant pro Fayen announced to the Head Pro that he wished to go on vacation in the fall, when the busy season would be over.

The Head Pro asked, "Where are you going?"

Fayen said, "Around on pilgrimage."

"What is the purpose of pilgrimage?" the Head Pro asked.

Fayen said, "I don't know."

The Head Pro said, "Not knowing is nearest."

—*Zen golf koan*

234

Pilgrim's Progress: Golfing Nepal

JUST AS YOU EXIT THE INTERNATIONAL AIRPORT IN KATH-mandu, Nepal—after piling your bags into a rickshaw and watching the skinny umber legs of the driver pumping at the bicycle pedals as he takes you toward the heart of the dark city, when the smoky heat and smudged brown sky of the third world have begun hinting that you're not in Connecticut anymore, that you've traveled beyond the borders of comfort and familiarity and toilets with seats (or toilets at all)—you will spot a vaguely familiar sight beyond the weeds growing up through the asphalt of the crumbling tarmac. You'll have to ignore the cows and water buffalo wandering the burnt grass for a meal, and it will certainly help to use your imagination and to alter your subjective perceptions, but that expanse of rolling hills and scorched terrain *is* a golf course. That it is one of the first things you see in Nepal—before the snowy teeth of the Himalayas, before the teeming, ancient streets of Kathmandu—might appear to some golfers as a very clear sign, although exactly what it is a sign of may seem less certain. But surely you'll recognize it as another golf koan.

And while that course may connect you at least tenuously to the ordered world you left behind just twenty-seven hours ago via a cramped airline seat beside a wailing baby and a portly Jehovah's Witness, by its very difference from every golf course you've ever seen it will also warn you that your own universe has shifted more than slightly off center, as if you've drunk too many cocktails, or just awakened from one of those dreams where you're naked in public, or being chased by monsters, and you wake up with the sheets soaked in sweat.

The country of Nepal is rather short on golf courses, al-though it *is* home to several of the planet's highest mountains, as well as some extremely vengeful intestinal parasites. Not long ago, I undertook a kind of pilgrimage to Nepal, a journey beyond the familiar, to see those mountains and to play golf in the company of two old friends: Dave Kleiber, a frenetic, tireless, single-minded humanist with a very consistent iron game, who was finishing a two-year stint in the Peace Corps overseeing forestry projects in Nepal's dry Terrai region, and John Hayden, powerfully built, Nordically handsome, intense and yet relaxed in a spiritual way (though known to miss some very short putts), who had arranged a thirty-day leave from his job selling computer systems for Hewlett Packard in Seattle. I was on assignment for a magazine, and prefer not to talk about my own golf game anymore—my privilege as the journalist.

The three of us hadn't been together for more than two years, since we'd all lived in Portland, Oregon, at a point in our lives when we were searching for something that we all understood but none of us could articulate. As part of our reunion itinerary, and as a nod to the lazy late-summer afternoons when we'd played lush green courses together after work, we arranged our Nepal adventure so that we could golf once or twice in the shadow of the Himalayas.

It wasn't the actual golf so much as the *idea* of the golf that seemed so full of potential. For one thing, I was curious to see if the spirit of the game, the true, palpitating green heart of golf, would thrive so far beyond familiar borders, in such completely unmanicured terrain. This trip was a field test of my growing belief that it was in exactly such places that golf assumed deeper context and best expressed its mystery. There was something about our traveling so far—both to play golf in such a surreal location, and to walk up into the highest mountains on earth—that made the trip feel ripe for revelation.

I also figured that our particular golf would absorb meaning by serving as a ritual of reunion and convocation, a celebration of our coming together again. I hoped that it might connect us to who we'd been—both as individuals and as friends—back in Portland, and that it might reflect who we were now and where each of us was along the path of our larger journeys. Years from now, if John and Dave and I find ourselves together for even a little while, we'll have something to talk about—or *not* talk about—that is uniquely ours. Golf, like the most adventurous travel, provides a means of connection.

In some ways it seemed such a silly thing, the golfing. And yet discovery requires unusual effort, and sometimes doing something patently impractical and just plain bizarre opens us to unexpected possibilities.

On our first afternoon in Kathmandu, Dave acted as if we'd just driven over from a neighboring town—which is to say it never occurred to him (ever, in any circumstance) that we might be tired. After allowing us to drop our backpacks at the White Lotus Guest House, where he'd rented a room, Dave led us on a climb up through the winding streets of the city to visit the monkey temple and perhaps glean our first view of the mountains we'd come so far to see. From the stone promontory of the temple, with monkeys prowling around us like bearded anorexics, we looked out over the smoking city tumbling haphazardly across the plain. But the mountains—camouflaged by haze—stood invisible beyond the distant blue horizon line, protected from sight by the thick, palpable sky. To see what lay hidden behind the grayness would require a difficult journey, as it often does.

We spent two more days amid the expatriate escapism of Kathmandu, sipping drinks in bars crowded with hip Westerners, combing the shops of the Thamel district for yak-wool sweaters and silver-and-turquoise jewelry, dreaming of the Himalayas, and joking about golf. Since our various intestinal problems hadn't struck yet, we ate huge breakfasts of huevos rancheros, pancakes, and banana-nut muffins in the garden at Mike's American Café and talked of our lives.

After those first lost days in Kathmandu sloughing off jet lag, we were anxious to leave for the mountains. Dave had planned—and I use the word loosely—a trekking route through the Kanchenjunga region, which had opened to foreigners only a month before. It would, he promised, give us a chance to see a part of Nepal that hadn't been ruined by the kind of travelers who demanded clean hotels and cold Cokes. Although I saw absolutely nothing wrong with either clean hotels or cold Cokes, I agreed that it sounded like a grand adventure. Our final destination, and the high point of our journey, would be the base camp of Kanchenjunga Peak, at 16,000 feet. But before we started gaining altitude, we'd travel across the flat, arid Terrai region for the singular and ludicrous purpose of playing a round of golf in Darhan. Why? We had no idea.

We began by flying from Kathmandu to a small town called Biratnagar. If the capital of Nepal had seemed beyond the fairway, in Biratnagar we entered a realm of thick rough. Along the road from the airport into town, brown faces stared out at us from wooden shacks, from the porches of houses already falling back into piles of bricks, from behind the veils of pink and green saris. Beggars and holy men (it was difficult to distinguish between them), women with gold rings in their noses, and children wearing filthy T-shirts gazed at us with our heavy, multicolored packs.

We spent that night in the Hotel Himalaya, where a ceiling fan pushed the mosquitoes around the room as if they were on a ride at Disneyland (John was sure that he recognized one of them from the White Lotus Guest House in Kathmandu), and the bathroom floor was like a dance hall for a cotillion of football-shaped bugs with many legs. We ate a big Indian meal that left me with a case of tandoori stomach—just a preview of things to come—and listened to a brass band playing out in the street.

In the morning, we rode on the bus from Biratnagar to Darhan—and I mean *on* the bus, clinging to suitcases and bags of rice that had been strapped to the roof and trying not to disturb the goats or crush the bamboo cages full of ducklings. For the duration of the two-hour ride through dusty villages, we sucked diesel fumes and listened to the copilot banging on the side of the overcrowded bus to inform the driver that he had enough room to pass a cow or that somebody wished to get off. In Darhan, we walked through the kiln-hot village with full packs on, dreaming of the cool salve of the mountains, and asking startled Nepalis if they knew where the clubhouse was.

The golf course in Darhan was memorable even while it lacked some of the traditional amenities, such as grass. It had been built by the British on what was once an army outpost for training Gurkha soldiers, but which had been converted to a Nepali medical school. It seemed so like the British to hack a golf course out of harsh terrain, making this blowy desert seem just a little more like the green, gorse-covered landscapes of home.

239

The best part of golfing in Darhan was the blooming jacaranda trees, which looked like bright purple puffs of smoke against the dry brown landscape. But the course had other original touches as well. For example, it is among the very few golf venues in the world where you can actually *rent* golf balls and bargain over the price of your greens fees. Of the billions of golf balls manufactured by Spalding and other companies over the past decades, none of the new ones had made it yet to Nepal.

Nobody else was out on the course that day we played; in fact, nobody was out at all, and the pro had to be fetched from some cool, dry place where any sensible person might have been hiding from the sun.

The two caddies assigned to wheel our bags along the dirt fairways actually seemed pleased to be going out with us, and they behaved with grave formality—solemnly handing us the correct clubs and speaking in an encouraging and continuous manner, although John and I couldn't understand a word they said.

The fact that there wasn't a blade of grass to be found on the Darhan golf course, and that the tattered flags were limp in the heat, sometimes made it difficult to determine where the greens were. On the fourth hole, which doglegged left just beyond the water buffalo, John was peering into the flat distance trying to make out where he should hit.

One of the caddies, who seemed to have taken a respectful liking to John, imitated the way he held his hand above his eyes to shield the sun.

"Panni tanki," the caddy said.

John looked at him and said, "Panni tanki?"

The caddy smiled at their sudden ability to communicate.

"Panni tanki," he said again, nodding vigorously. He handed John a long iron and looked off toward some distant point.

John addressed his ball with great deliberation before hitting in the wrong direction, a hundred yards or so beyond a fence enclosing somebody's cow pasture. His caddy found this hysterical.

John called to Dave, who'd already hit his second shot predictably close to the pin, "What does *panni tanki* mean?"

"Water tower," Dave said, pointing at the huge one just behind the green.

"Panni tanki," the caddy reiterated, nodding his head.

We were wrung out and dehydrated after nine holes, and John was upset that he'd lost one of his rental balls—not because of the money, but more out of a sense of having let the pro down—so we decided to quit and take a rickshaw back to the bus station in town. After the traditional Nepali bus-boarding ritual of shouting and tugging at the other passengers, we happily took our seats on top of the bus for the ride to Hele, from where we'd begin the second stage of our pilgrimage: the trek into the Himalayas.

> The only Zen you find on the tops of mountains is the Zen you bring up there.
> —*Robert Pirsig,* Zen and the Art of Motorcycle Maintenance

This bus ride was spectacular, right up through the heart of the hills rising out of the dusty flats. We sped past houses clinging to the steep slopes along a ribbon of road that nearly curled back on itself over and over as we climbed. The air grew cool as we ascended, and the road crested and rolled down into a valley where whitewater flowed in the riverbed

241

and the surrounding country flew by in a broken topography of bright green rice paddies divided by gray stone walls. In the distance, still, no mountains were visible.

Hele—where John taught a group of local children to dance the hokey-pokey—was literally at the end of the road, and I liked the idea of having followed pavement for as far as it would go, and then continuing under our own power up toward the high peaks. Over the next ten days we climbed through forests of rhododendron blooming pink and red, their petals strewn along the trail by mountain winds. One afternoon we came upon an elderly man walking the other way who proudly displayed two cheap chrome watches on his wrist, a status symbol even though neither one worked—which was fine because he probably couldn't tell time anyway and likely had few appointments to keep. We passed through dozens of tiny hillside villages where we bought hot milk tea and packaged coconut biscuits and occasionally spent the night in the dark back rooms of villagers' homes.

It rained on us for at least an hour or two every day, and even when it wasn't raining the sky remained leaden with storm clouds. By the time we'd climbed up to a town called Taplejung, which was modern enough to have occasional electricity and two hotels, John and I were ready to slow down and catch our breath. This was our *vacation*, we reminded each other; we weren't prisoners of war.

So we holed up in a tiny hotel room decorated with magazine photos of Michael Jackson and Sylvester Stallone. That first evening, I walked down the cobbled street behind our room and from the covered porch of a Buddhist temple watched a violent thunderstorm rumbling through the steep

242

valley below us. Out there somewhere, I thought, hidden in clouds, were the high peaks we'd come so far to see.

The storm continued for three days, and so we hung tight in Taplejung, gorging ourselves on salty chow mein—the only dish served in the hotel restaurant—and playing cards in tea shops where the rain beat staccato rhythms on the tin roofs and the local men crowded around to observe us. By the time we left town during a very temporary lull in the weather, it was too late to make for the Kanchenjunga base camp, so we amended our plans and headed for a 12,000-foot summit that was capped by the Hindu pilgrimage site of Pathi, and which promised striking views of the mountains if the weather broke. It seemed a fitting destination, although the religious aspect of our own journey was of a completely different nature: continuous, without such a predetermined goal.

Our day-and-a-half trek up to the shrine at Pathi was cold and wet and difficult. Altitude stole our oxygen, rain ran under our waterproof jackets, hailstones stung our faces, and we spent a restless night in a cowshed trying to convince the cows to stay outside. When we finally reached the summit, clouds hung low over the mountains and visibility was about twenty feet. The shelter we'd been told of turned out to be a half-covered goatshed, but there was some dry wood inside, and we built a fire against the damp chill. For the rest of the day we read thick novels, played cards, and wrote in our journals, enjoying the insular safety of riding out a storm in the company of friends.

A few hours later, the first group of dripping pilgrims arrived with their goats. When they'd finished rearranging our fire and spitting in the corners, these Hindus walked farther up the path to the shrine itself. We heard the myriad temple bells ringing loudly and the goats bleating, and then it was silent until the pilgrims returned with headless animals and began singeing off the hair in our fire and cooking their sacrificial meal.

John and I slept in the tent that night to escape the constant coughing of twenty wet Nepalis. We left Dave—who at least spoke their language—to stake out a dry corner for our gear. Somewhere in the middle of a languorous Caribbean dream, John woke me because the tent was collapsing from the weight of new-fallen snow. I nodded as he explained this to me, to imply that I understood what he was talking about.

"Panni tanki," I said before dropping back into a sound sleep until morning.

The precipitation continued on and off, as did the parade of pilgrims, who arrived in groups of ten or twelve, rang the bells, slaughtered a few goats, and then disappeared back into the fog.

By our final evening at Pathi, I could barely stand the smell of burning goat hair in the shed, so I climbed the hundred yards up to the top of the mountain for some fresh air. The rain had stopped for a little while, and the muted light shone brighter than it had since our arrival. From the windswept summit I could for the first time make out a forested ridge just across the valley, and, a moment later, another ridge rising behind it in continuing premonition.

Clouds slipped quickly across the deep void below me like fleeing ghosts. The color of the horizon shifted from pearl gray to a wispy ivory. Then the heavy sky broke and scattered, and I felt the sudden rushing momentum of change. Where a view of high-piled white clouds had stubbornly held its position way above me in the distance, I now realized that the whiteness had relented, giving way to another, different whiteness—of

snow-covered peaks, mottled by dark granite outcroppings—
and that I was receiving my long-awaited, knee-weakening
look at the Himalayan range.

I stood slack with wonder for the next forty-five minutes
as mountain winds funneled clouds out of the valley. The sky
blued, revealing that those first peaks, which seemed so enor-
mously high, were only a ridge of false summits, as were the
next set to appear, and the next—like the kind of small, intermittent revelations you experience on the way toward enlightenment. For a few moments the sky cleaved open like a
split watermelon, spilling peaks in every direction. I saw the
tops of Kanchenjunga, Kumba Karma, and dozens more; way
off in the distance, I glimpsed a familiar-shaped peak that rose
above all the others: Everest.

John and Dave and a group of young Nepalis had come up
on the promontory, and we watched mesmerized, unspeaking,
united in our awe. I felt the mountains transferring something
to me, as if they were radioactive, as if the exposure were
rearranging the molecules that composed me, as if I would
never, ever be the same again.

And then the peaks were gone. Clouds shut them in like a
curtain closing on some fantastical exhibit. Darkness fell. Night
came on.

The next morning we hiked back down to the mountain
airport at Taplejung and began the trip back to Kathmandu to
complete the final stage of this part of our pilgrimage.

The python was not in his cage beside the first tee at the
Gokarna Safari Golf Club, just outside of Kathmandu, when
we played there after returning from the mountains. I searched

for him quite thoroughly as John and Dave and two other Peace Corps volunteers stretched and warmed up and compared digestive tract disorders. Trying to appear casual as I looked for the six-foot-long snake, I thought, "This is not a good omen."

And so began the first (and only) Gastrointestinal Challenge, a nine-hole competition in which just finishing felt as good as a tour win, and where John enjoyed a major advantage because he got sick off the upper deck of the clubhouse *before* the round even began. The rest of us played under the pressure of knowing that at any moment—perhaps in the middle of a perfect backswing—we might have to make a run for the bushes, a kind of sport in its own right for visitors to Nepal.

But the links at Gokarna were memorable for many reasons totally unrelated to digestion. As if the setting amid a ramshackle third-world village weren't strange enough, the golf course was home to a zooful of animals, some of whom wandered freely across the fairways and greens: rhesus monkeys, who scampered about like fur-covered toddlers; lithe gazelles watching for errant shots from the rough, a horned gallery; elephants hanging around the nineteenth hole like familiar fat men who won't go home.

Our caddies, whose combined ages were probably still ten years less than my own and I'm not even thirty yet (okay, I'm thirty-four), enjoyed laughing at our bad golf shots even more than the monkeys did. They loved to practice their English by saying words such as *jungle* and *leech pond* when we inquired about where our drives had gone. Still, they were quite handy for yelling in Nepali at the picnickers who were eating lunch in the middle of several different fairways and no doubt wondering what in the world *we* were doing.

Which is an excellent question, and one that I can only answer by saying that it is not the target but the arrow in flight, never the destination and always the journey that resonates with meaning, because our lives are only—and nothing but—a pilgrimage.

CHAPTER SIXTEEN

High Places

The Head Pro asked, "Atop a thousand-foot elevated tee box, how do you step forward?"

One of his assistants answered, "One who stands atop a thousand-foot elevated tee box may have gained initiation, but this is not yet reality. Atop a thousand-foot elevated tee box, one should step forward to manifest the whole body throughout the universe."

—Zen golf koan

Why is death so much on my mind when I do not feel I am afraid of it?—the dying, yes . . . but not the state itself. And yet I cling—to what? What am I to make of these waves of timidity, this hope of continuity when at other moments I feel free as the bharal [sheep] on those heights, ready for wolf and snow leopard alike? I must be careful, that is true, for I have . . . much work to finish; but these aren't honest reasons, past a

248

point. Between clinging and letting go, I feel a
terrific struggle. This is a fine chance to let go,
to "win my life by losing it," which means not
recklessness but acceptance, not passivity but
nonattachment.

—*Peter Mathiessen,* The Snow Leopard

T HE EIGHTEENTH HOLE AT THE LAWRENCE GOLF CLUB ON
Long Island—where I played a lot of golf when I was just
out of school—is a tough, classical finishing hole, and one of
my all-time favorites. But what makes it a great hole isn't the
sparkling bay running along the left side, sprinkled with yachts
and lined with expensive homes; nor is it the manner in which
the fairway draws your eye around toward the clubhouse (and
bar) the way a landscape painting leads you into and then out
of a pastoral scene. The eighteenth at Lawrence is an awesome
golf hole because it's designed to teach a clear lesson about
the relationship between risk and reward—and, necessarily,
to reveal something about every golfer by the way he chooses
to play the hole.

The ideal tee shot on eighteen should come to rest on a
peninsula of land that extends out into the choppy blue water
of the bay. Approximately three hundred yards from the tee,
on the far side of that peninsula, the bay curls around and
narrows to a thin finger that points to the right across the
entire fairway, which itself doglegs to the left. The closer to
the water that you play your drive, the shorter your second
shot to the green. But since most golfers have a tendency to
slice, to land in the "A" position, you'd have to aim out over
the water and let your ball fade back toward safer ground.

Or you can choose—as I often do—to face the challenging
risk/reward scenario on your second shot. I usually aim my

drive at the left edge of the fairway, and my slice curves it safely away from the water, but occasionally far enough away that I'm faced with this dilemma on my approach (if it hasn't gone too far, into a thin line of trees): Do I lay up to the water's edge and play for bogey, or take out my three wood and swing hard enough to loosen my dental work in an attempt to fly the hazard (and a couple of gnarly sand traps) and blast one onto the green—a shot that requires total faith, transcendence of negative thoughts, perfect mechanics, maybe 230 yards of carry, and a prevailing wind?

Although I've knocked my fair share of golf balls into that water, I never really stop to consider my options for very long. I already know what the smart play is, but I'm not out on the golf course to show off my IQ. There, in most circumstances, I'd much rather risk severe consequences for the possibility of glory than shoot for a conservative five, which might make me an exciting scramble partner, if not a very reliable stockbroker. I always try to grab my three wood before I have time to think consciously about what I'm doing; although I'd probably still reach for the same club after weighing my choices, the act of reflection can make the water seem wider than it already is. This, for me, is the hole's lesson: If you don't take a chance, there's no possibility of something fantastic happening.

Zen golf is largely about transcending fear and subjectivism and self-consciousness and daring to take the kinds of shots that might lead to a good score on the eighteenth at Lawrence. But beyond the fairway, Zen golf is also about living in a particular way and manifesting an active, individualistic, flexible, inquisitive, and sometimes daring vision of the world through everything that you do. It's about using golf as a way of transporting yourself to a new dimension, gaining access to new perspectives, and maybe racking up a few birdies along the way.

Many of the reasons for traveling beyond the fairway—physically, metaphorically, and metaphysically—and for taking the risks to reach unmanicured terrain, should be clear: Such a path may lead toward enlightenment or otherwise improve and expand the range of your experiences. But now that we've moved outward toward the distant edges of the rough, to a point where further movement may require abandoning awareness of the very fairways we've moved out from, it's important to consider the inherent risks, to address the metaphorical equivalent of what it might mean to knock a ball into the water or over a cliff. And to think about whether, in some circumstances, the risks so far outweigh any possible rewards that it might be worth playing a bit more conservatively—if not on the fairway, then at least beyond it.

Dangers actually lurk on both sides of the fairway. On one side lies the kind of manic, obsessive golf in which every bad shot drives us into anger and frustration and disappointment. On the opposite side lies the danger of letting go of such things too successfully, of transcending so entirely that we lose sight of our place in the world, of traveling so far into the zone that we can't come back—as happened to Captain Kurtz, for example, and to a friend of mine in college who took too much LSD.

Spontaneity, transcendence, and the ability to push beyond limits encompasses a dark back country, too, rendering this edge dangerous, suppressing our migration. Moving beyond the familiar involves abandoning the very reasons behind limitations—reasons of safety, sanity, and order. We must risk losing control in order to experience the ecstasy of discovery and enlightenment, but it's always possible—and must be so—that we'll lose something in the process.

Zen ultimately offers a centered, balanced, and harmonious path that winds between such extremes, a place where opposites converge into Oneness. While this may seem to contradict the notion of moving further and further into unmanicured terrain, it also embraces this idea in a way that can't be fully understood in purely rational terms. Put more simply—as a sort of koan—you must travel beyond the fairway to travel better down the fairway, just as you must swing easy to hit your drive far; just as you must give up wanting to score well to be able ever to score well. Such are the paradoxes of Zen golf.

Because most people inhabit territory closer to landmarks of obsession and control than of transcendence, Zen may appear to involve only movement in the direction of transcendence. But as you become more successful in moving beyond the fairway, the possibility of going too far toward that other, spontaneous edge increases.

To exercise healthy transcendence and spontaneity, therefore, we must develop something inside us that will prove powerful enough to recognize that moment when we may be on the verge of going too far, that we'll know when it's time to plant our flag, define the outermost reaches of the territory we can visit, and accept the limits of our own range.

Some people never recognize that moment. Some people hike out along the steep arête between challenge and self-destructiveness, between reward and risk. They slice thin slivers of daring until the knife scrapes bone. They always shoot for the pin.

252

Some people transcend and speed past even the last mile-post, the final yard marker indicating that beyond lies inescapable danger, a place where risk finally fails to offer anything but the most fleeting and illusory reward. Regardless of your personal philosophy, in some circumstances—such as in the metaphorical equivalent of not being able to reach the green on your second shot on the eighteenth at Lawrence Golf Club—it may be worth putting metaphorical implications aside and simply laying up.

Nirvana is not in itself the goal of Zen Buddhism, but a temporary resting place on an endless pathway of complete realization. [The Master's commentary summarizes] . . . the danger of overestimating the experience of quiescent nirvana and mistaking a means for the end. Slightly more concealed is the parallel message that there are counterfeit and genuine versions of nirvana. It is not only the counterfeit nirvana (quietism or nihilism) that "blinds" the unwary seeker, but even the real nirvana also blinds people when it is taken out of context as an expedient method and turned into an object of devotion as if it were an ultimate goal.

—*Thomas Cleary, translator's comments in* No Barrier: Unlocking the Zen Koan

A couple of years ago I had a very bad winter while living in Oregon; it seemed to rain nearly every day for months, and by March I found myself craving some sort of impractical, spontaneous activity that might propel me beyond the narrow confines of my own soggy fairways. Golf was not an option due to the weather, so I sought some other way of pursuing my metaphor of moving beyond boundaries and limitations. I

253

sought to pursue Zen golf beyond the sport of golf, itself. I might have chosen virtually any activity: skiing or flower arranging, scuba diving or archery. I could have sought to follow this path by the way I drove my car. But I decided upon a solo adventure in the wilderness.

So I bought some backpacking supplies—even though I'd never gone backpacking before—and drove my ailing Toyota south for fifteen hundred miles, to the hot, dry heart of the Utah desert. I parked on the edge of a scrub-covered mesa thirty miles by dirt road from the nearest town, and hiked down into wilderness canyons for six days, through a landscape so hauntingly beautiful, so unlike anything I'd ever seen before, that at times I felt I'd completely lost myself.

On my fourth morning out, I woke early and filled my daypack for a long hike up to the rim of the canyon more than a thousand feet above the confluence of the streambed I'd been hiking along and the river it emptied into. But in the process of traversing the steep slopes of dunes and talus toward that rim, I suddenly became confused by metaphor: I was climbing *up* toward the edge of something, rather than out laterally and beyond it. This unsettled me until I recognized that the very structure of my metaphor—of any metaphor (such as the notion of moving beyond the fairway)—is itself worth pushing beyond. In fact, I realized that such metaphors *must* eventually be transcended: a realization that may have saved my life.

After two hours of climbing, all at once the canyon fell away behind me and I took a last upward step onto the rim. I spun slowly around to view the Kaipairowitz Plateau and the Henry Mountains rising along the distant blue horizons. On the edge of those remote and mysterious canyonlands, I felt deeply grateful for having chosen the unlikely option of coming there. I wanted to cry out, so I loosed a long and breathless yell that chilled me with its utter, limitless transcendence.

In this moment I drifted out onto a small peninsula of rock that extended over the canyon like an open palm. I stood very close to the edge on its chafed fingertips and looked straight down to the Escalante River flowing the color of wheat beer a thousand feet below.

I had traveled a long way from the heart of the familiar, from the center of the fairway, from this journey's origins in Zen and golf, to a landscape so bizarre and captivating, to a place so remote, to an edge so palpable that it was no longer a mere analogy for outward movement. It was the thing itself, and confronting it I knew I was straddling the border between darkness and light, that I'd found one place where all opposites converged.

Standing on that ledge of warm rock I realized that this notion of pushing beyond limitations, that this metaphorical road I'd been traveling, led right to this place and this moment where, faced with the outermost landmark of transcendence and spontaneity, following my metaphor any farther meant going too far.

I suddenly believed that to experience the ultimate release and most complete freedom; to attain unrestrained enlightenment; to ascend the heights of Crazy Cloud Zen; to meld with the universe as I'd hoped to accomplish through golf and philosophy and other forms of adventure, meant spontaneously throwing myself down from the rim toward the muddy river before I could think about implications. I was as far out as I'd ever been, and the joy of it was so immense that I wanted only to take the next step. I *wanted* to jump because it seemed to symbolize a commitment to living, if only for a moment, without holding anything back.

In transcending consciousness to perform our best, we must—with an abiding faith—let go of the very control that might be keeping us safe, and maybe even alive. Which leads me to believe that a kind of reckless misperception must arise for some people from the sense of what is possible, a misperception that causes them to want so much from their lives that they're willing to unhook the safety net of their own self-preserving instincts, to ignore their own final mileposts, and leap out into a void of pure mystery and potential as giddily intoxicating as oxygen. Perhaps this explains how some mountain climbers die, pushing forward when they know to turn back from the peak; how some scuba divers—caught in the gripping ecstasy of nitrogen narcosis—recognize the danger but continue to descend.

In the realm of metaphor, gravity is negotiable. For someone who has mistaken the metaphorical for the actual, who has forgotten that we create analogies not to live in them but to help us live better in the real world, cliff walls fly past quickly in red-orange streaks, and the ground rises up too fast.

I stopped myself on the very edge of the canyonlands and accepted that limit not because I was afraid of jumping, but simply because I didn't want to die. A road is just a road, and we all have choices. Those choices mark the route of our journeys like stone cairns along a remote trail, and they determine the people we become. But it is that process of *becoming* that matters most.

Regardless of which Zen vehicle you choose to help you along the path, extremes of spontaneity and transcendence may appear at certain moments to represent a final destination, the ultimate move beyond the fairway; but making that particular leap is to forget that the true journey is infinite, and has no end.

After a few more minutes on the rim, I began the slow descent back to my waterside campsite, back inward a step or two toward the fairway, thinking that merely by having risked this trip to an unlikely precipice above the Escalante River, and by backing away, I'd already propelled myself outward a little closer toward a different and far more enlightening—if ultimately unreachable—edge.

Acknowledgments

Although only one person writes a book like this, literally hundreds of others make it a possibility. In traveling to resorts and golf courses on four continents, I've been fortunate enough to receive the support, time, good wishes, generosity, stories and personal feelings, as well as a thousand other gifts from golfers, hotel staff, public relations experts, travel agents, airlines, and countless others who believed in this project, and many of whom helped defray costs without knowing for sure if the book would ever come to be. This is their book, too. I wish I could thank every one of them personally, from deep in my heart and beyond my own fairway, but for now, the following—though incomplete—will have to do.

My trip to Scotland could not have occurred without the tenacious, meticulous, good-natured, and over-generous aid of

ACKNOWLEDGMENTS

Tom Liszewski, President of Golf Vacations, in Boston, MA. On that trip, many golf courses and hotels were generous enough to host me. I'd also like to thank Mr. C. J. Rouse, General Manager of the Turnberry Hotel and Golf Course, and Ewen Bowman, Golf Operations Manager; David Donaldson, Secretary of Prestwick Golf Club; Martyn Huish, Assistant Pro at North Berwick Golf Club; the Assistant Secretary of Gullane Golf Club; Nan Hay, at Carnoustie Championship Links; Mr. James Somerville, Peter Gordon, and friends at Nairn Golf Club; and Mr. Ian Walker, Secretary of Royal Dornoch. I'm also grateful to Rick Mears, of Lou Hammond and Associates, and Guy Crawford, General Manager, for arranging my most excellent stay at Edinburgh's fantastic Balmoral Hotel, and to Mr. Peter Atherton, Director and General Manager of the Kingsmills Hotel in Inverness. Thanks also go out to Bedford Pace, of the British Tourist Authority, and John Lampl, who availed British Airways' awesomely comfortable service.

For lodging in Alaska, I am grateful to the Wasilla Lake Bed and Breakfast; Richards House B&B in Fairbanks; Marion Nelson of the Kenai Merit Inn in Kenai; Wayne and Marilyn Burkhart, the patient hosts with the most astounding view in Alaska at their Glacier House B&B in Palmer; Ken and Judy Marlow, hosts at the lovely backcountryish Marlow's Kenai River B&B in Soldotna; Mike and Sue Wilson, for the gorgeous suite, panoramic view, and excellent cappuccino at their Forget Me Not Lodge in Fairbanks; and Judy Trotter, hostess extraordinaire, who willingly dined, entertained, and comforted me at the fabulously architected and decorated Swan House B&B in Anchorage.

As for help with arrangements, thanks to David Karp, Director of the Kenai Peninsula Tourism Marketing Council;

Suzi Bock, Tourism Director of the Matanuska-Susitna Convention and Visitors' Board; Ken Morris, Anchorage Convention and Visitor's Bureau; Britt Lively, Executive Director of the Palmer Economic Development Authority; and Mike Liebing.

And thanks most of all to my great golf hosts who put up with my mediocre play late into the night: Mark Dolesji at the Palmer Golf Course; Jack Stallings of the Northstar Golf Course; Dave Curwen and Lynn Immel, Fairbanks Golf Association; Mike Gould, Course Manager of the Chena Bend Golf Club, Fairbanks; Pat Cowan of Birch Ridge Golf Course in Soldotna; John McBride and George Collum at Moose Run Golf Course; Bob Nelson and Spike at Anchorage Golf Course; Don Morgan, Assistant Manager of the Kenai Golf Course.

Special thanks, too, to Al Olivetto and Robin at Delta Airlines, who were extremely generous with their time and help defraying airline costs under difficult and hurried circumstances. Everyone at Thai Airways (particularly Clause Jenson), and Surapon Fvetasreni at the Thai Tourism Board. Lew Smither III, Heidi Rush, Ramona Hurley, Alexandra Shontz, Dawn Mercer, and Sue Knight at the Innisbrook Golf Institute. Bill Johnson and Peter Jacobsen at the Fred Meyer Challenge. Charlie Greene at Duke's Lakeview Challenge. The staff at the Sahalee Golf Course in Clackamas, Oregon. Peter Martin and the Whiteface Inn and Resort. Karen Hoffman, George Rachani, Robert Tholl, and my many African hosts in Côte d'Ivoire. Mike Sullivan, Joe Stiefel, and Mike Ferris at Spalding, as well as Glenn Mastro of the Sherry Group.

I'd also like to offer special thanks to my agents, Ling Lucas and Ed Vesneske, Jr., for their patience, business expertise,

ACKNOWLEDGMENTS

and the original notion that I should think about writing a golf book. And to Leslie Meredith, Executive Editor, and Brian Tart, Assistant Editor, at Bantam Books for their excellent editorial help and guidance.

Finally, deep gratitude to Bob, Keith, Patti, Lauren, Wolf, Alex, Susan, Mildred, and Sherri—they know what for. And to David Fishman, Hope Edelman, Dave Gould, Joe Passov, Leon Werdinger, John Hayden, Dave Kleiber, and Sue Hill for all their help, support, and encouragement.

About the Author

Jeff Wallach is a writer and journalist specializing in golf, travel, outdoor adventure/recreation, and environmental issues. His work has appeared widely in such magazines as *Golf*, *Golf Illustrated*, *Golf Digest*, *National Golfer*, *Sierra*, *Men's Fitness*, *Rodale's Scuba Diving*, *Town and Country*, *Money*, *Discover*, *Diversion*, and many others. He is also the Associate Editor of *America's Greatest Resorts*, and a contributing writer for *Petersen's Golfing*. The author holds a Bachelor's in English from Vassar College and a Master's in Writing from Brown University. Although a mediocre golfer, he claims to hit long drives for a journalist.

796.352 W155
Wallach, Jeff.
Beyond the fairway : Zen
lessons, insights, and
AUG 3 0 2006

9 780553 373332